Could Hertfordshire Business School become central to the local business ecosystem?

RESEARCH PROJECT

Bogdan Ciocoiu

MBA – University of Hertfordshire Business School

May 2019

TABLE OF CONTENTS

EXECUTIVE SUMMARY

This research paper analyses Hertfordshire's local business community and establishes what changes Hertfordshire Business School should operate to its business model so that it shifts to the centre of its local business community. In doing so, the research looks at existing literature defining local business ecosystems and business communities, while establishing what components and members are constructing such environments. During this phase, the paper establishes the relationship between the existing parts of the ecosystem, and it associates any power relations between them with theory and literature. The project will also consult existing literature to establish current business models which Hertfordshire Business School can undertake to deliver their objective of becoming central to the local business community.

During the research phase, the project identifies the contributions brought by each significant stakeholder from the local business community, including the influence excerpted by Hertfordshire Business School. At the analysis and conclusion stages, the research project combines its findings and makes recommendations concerning business model changes Hertfordshire Business School could undertake to secure a more central role within the local business community.

This paper aims to contribute to the existing literature by expanding it with information about Hertfordshire Business School and its role within Hertfordshire business community by providing information about the traits sought by local businesses of various sizes and how the academic institution could leverage those, increase its visibility and value and reposition itself in the centre of the business ecosystem.

GLOSSARY

ACRONYM	DESCRIPTION
HBS	Hertfordshire Business School
BA	Business and administration
ONS	Office for National Statistics
DE	Department for Education
UCAS	Universities and Colleges Admissions Service
SME	Subject Matter Experts
LEP	Local Enterprise Partnership
KPI	Key Performance Indicator
CMDA	Chartered Manager Degree Apprenticeship
CABS	Chartered Association of Business Schools
USP	Unique Selling Point

INTRODUCTION

The University of Hertfordshire is the most prominent academic institution located in South Hertfordshire having two large campuses and 12 schools including Hertfordshire Business School ("HBS") (University of Hertfordshire, 2019), delivering 269 academic Bachelors and Masters courses every year (UCAS, 2018). Alongside the teaching activities, a new educational trend emerged involving universities, well documented in the literature, encouraging business schools and learning providers to engage with local businesses as part of their academic programmes (Miller, 2019). The overarching objective of these interactions is to support the development of local companies and institutions, to provide students with industry work experience and to create opportunities for collaboration and innovation (McAdam and McAdam, 2019).

This research paper starts by exploring Hertfordshire's business ecosystem[1], will further analyse the external stakeholders influencing the business communities within the county and will aim to establish the characteristics of a business model that Hertfordshire Business School should undertake to become the central stakeholder within Hertfordshire's business ecosystem. In doing so, the research project will investigate several aspects including establishing what defines Herts' business community, analyse the relationships between businesses and local support institutions providing direction to organisations and will look at the benefits of maintaining a fluent collaboration between the main external stakeholders from within Hertfordshire and the business communities.

This paper documents a research project of a qualitative nature, and it will lead to the development of propositions. The project's underlying objective is to design a strategy and a business model that HBS can implement to become central to its local business ecosystem, by providing business knowledge and by advocating for innovation.

---

[1] A business ecosystem is a network of interlinked entities which includes businesses, which form interactions while supplying services or products specific to their value propositions (Letaifa et al., 2013)

The next section of the research project will analyse existing literature about Hertfordshire business community, including establishing its structure, dynamics and its most influential components. Also, the literature review will establish HBS' position within the business community, including its current contribution and will investigate what characteristics the business school must develop to become central to the community. The research project conducts primary research through interviews held with key representatives from the local business community to establish the relationship between HSB and local businesses. It concludes with the findings corroborated with industry papers and academic literature, providing a business model that aims to aid HBS with its transition to the centre of Hertfordshire local business community.

LITERATURE REVIEW

The purpose of the literature review is to find existing literature and industry articles regarding the project's aim and to pave the way for primary and secondary research to complement the initial findings so that conclusions can be drawn and recommendations will be made to allow HBS to achieve its objective. In continuation, this section will start by exploring the role of higher education institutions within the Hertfordshire business community and later will focus on HBS, while aiming to develop a target business model that will enable it to transition to a central position within the local business community. This section of the paper reviews the existing literature describing the business ecosystem (Lexicon.ft.com, 2019), detailing its structure, members and the contribution of its elements while aiming to establish how HBS should tailor their operating model to maximise its contribution and benefits brought to the business community.

COUNTY OF HERTFORDSHIRE

Hertfordshire is an East England county structured in 10 districts, neighbouring Greater London with a population of 1.16 million, of which 63.1% (circa 700,000) are at working age (Department for Education, 2017) and with 64,080 active businesses (Hertfordshire LEP, 2015), suggesting one resident in eleven has an invested interest within the local business community. Existing industry reports indicate that while neighbouring with Greater London, Buckinghamshire and Bedfordshire, Hertfordshire has embedded a high level of work ethic in terms of employment, micro businesses or lifestyle businesses (Forbes.com, 2019). This behavioural value originates from access to a broader and better-paid job market but also subjected to higher living costs associated with the Greater London area (Hertfordshire Ltd, 2017). There appears to be a decreased level of interest in undertaking more top education courses, therefore creating a certain level of competition on existing universities when it comes to attracting the remaining less-interested students (Network, 2019). Evidence shows universities are under pressure to offer more than just degrees, as they must adapt to new market demands and must engage in partnerships with local industries and the private sector to provide a better-prepared workforce to empower the local economy (Business, 2019). This research project will analyse the level of readiness and preparation at which HBS is for the above academic market tendencies and its level of involvement and embeddedness within its local Hertfordshire's business community.

BUSINESS ECOSYSTEM

Letaifa et al. (2013) define a business ecosystem as a network of interlinked entities which includes businesses, organisations, institutions, groups of firms, or similar individual and collective entities which form interactions while supplying services or products specific to their value propositions. Bischoff et al. (2017) define the geographical boundaries of a local business ecosystem at the county level; therefore, this paper will refer to and research the Hertfordshire business ecosystem. There are several categories of entities which are forming the local business ecosystem, these being local businesses of various sizes, institutions, non-governmental groups, non-profit organisations, third sector representatives, as well as buyers, resellers and consumers (Bischoff et al., 2017). Rothschild (2004) suggests a business ecosystem such as Hertfordshire's exists as a result of the constant interactions and linkages between the above elements which are exercising give-and-take or push-pull interactions, effectively exchanging services, products or benefits of financial means or other matters.　　　　　　　　　　，

The ecosystem is in a constant state of flux[2] due to external shaping factors (Marmol at al., 2015) which are excerpting pressures and are influencing the way entities interact, effectively reshaping the ecosystem (Collaborative business ecosystems and virtual enterprises, 2013). Chron (2019) exemplifies these influential factors to potentially originate from employment trends, business rates, political decisions, the policy issued by local or central administrations, the national and regional economy and other political, economic, social, technological, environmental or legal factors. Barro (2001) identifies a correlation between the prosperity of the local economy (measured in terms of employment and job seeking rates), and the efficiencies within the local business ecosystem such as access to a skilled labour market, general work ethic, quality of education, access to

---

[2] State of flux refers to a state of volatility and indicates something can change and reshape (Bischoff, 2017)

business networks, access to professional consulting services and others. The research finds that the shape of the local business community is deemed essential for the overall economic development of a country.

Rana et al. (2018) claim that although it is formed from a substantial number of entities known as external stakeholders interacting between themselves in patterns, the majority of these entities tend to revolve around the centre of the local business ecosystem which is again occupied by another influential external stakeholder. Deloitte Insights (2019) describes the core of the local business ecosystem as another entity or stakeholder which fuels and maintains the ecosystem's dynamics, by providing knowledge to the stakeholders who need it at most such as micro or small businesses, by advising for expansion to those who need to experience growth, by advocating for innovation and by providing general direction and steer (Karhiniemi, 2009).

Local businesses, collectively, represent another stakeholder from a local business ecosystem. Local companies also serve the catalyst of the local economy as they interact with most of the other stakeholders, including primarily with the centre of the ecosystem, to fulfil their needs (Tuccillo, 2002). Rothschild (2004) shows local businesses are likely to create linkages with entities they perceive to be the most helpful in their endeavours (i.e. support organisations, enablers and catalysts) and it is that one of these enabling entities, will most likely be deemed by the ecosystem as central. HBS seeks to secure a central position within Hertfordshire's local business community, and this research project will identify the main traits which the centre body of Hertfordshire business ecosystem should produce to serve the other entities, including the businesses revolving around its axis. Based on the above and the literature reviewed, as far as Hertfordshire's business ecosystem is concerned micro and small businesses collectively represent one of the most critical stakeholders of the local business community, as well as Hertfordshire Business School, due to their influence over the local economy. Therefore, they are investigated in more detail in the upcoming sections.

MICRO AND SMALL BUSINESSES IN HERTFORDSHIRE

Industry reports show that 87% of the operating businesses registered in Hertfordshire are classified as micro-businesses which is above the national average of 85%, suggesting a specific entrepreneurial ethic is predominant within the county of Hertfordshire (Department for Education, 2017). Official reports show micro and small-businesses combined form 97.4% of the total number of companies operating in the county (Department for Education, 2017), which means the relationships formed between local businesses and external stakeholders from the local business ecosystem are predominantly formed based on the needs associated with micro and small enterprises (Enterprise Research centre, 2018).

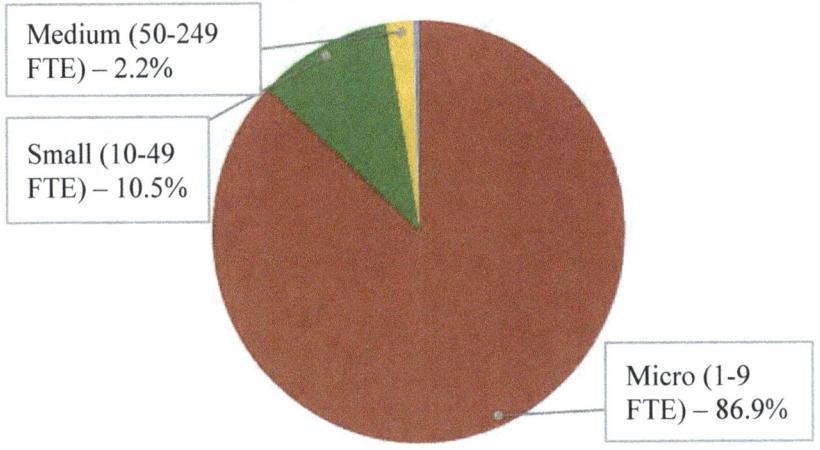

Medium (50-249 FTE) – 2.2%

Small (10-49 FTE) – 10.5%

Micro (1-9 FTE) – 86.9%

Figure 1: Proportion of micro organisations in Hertfordshire (Hertfordshire LEP, 2015)

The outstanding number of micro-businesses operating in Hertfordshire results from several stimulating factors such as support schemes and campaigns coordinated from both the central government (Gov.uk, 2018; Gov.uk-2, 2018; British Business Bank, 2018) and local learning providers (University of Hertfordshire, 2018) which have stimulated and contributed to the formation of an influential entrepreneurship culture within the county during past decades (Hertfordshire LEP, 2015). However, the

11

literature suggests that although there are organisations that increase the diversity of knowledge flows and provide support channels for start-ups and micro businesses in Hertfordshire, their contribution may not be fully aligned with what businesses need to experience long term growth (OECD. and Oecd Publishing, 1999; Carayannis et al., 2016). Bischoff et al. (2017) suggest efficient inner-stakeholder relationships are perceived as a success factor in steering entrepreneurship education by providing advice within the business community and information about industry best practices, therefore helping companies scale-up.

EXTERNAL STAKEHOLDERS

The literature reviewed did not reveal a one-stop-shop collection of information with an exhaustive list of details of Hertfordshire's external stakeholders listing their capabilities, alongside with all channels through which they support local entrepreneurs (Carayannis et al., 2018). However, the existing literature did provide several external stakeholders shown in figure 2, foreign to the local businesses but internal to the business ecosystem which contributes and invest in one way or another within the Hertfordshire business community.

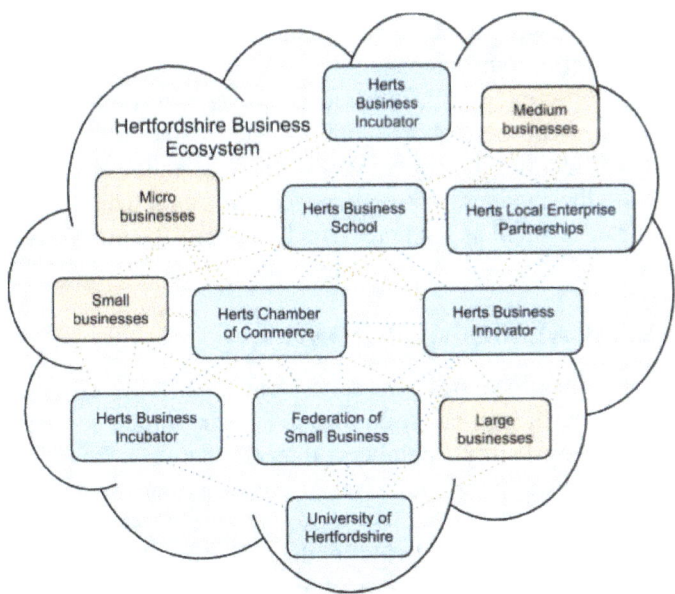

Figure 2: Hertfordshire business ecosystem (post-literature review)

For Hertfordshire's business ecosystem, the external stakeholders are Herts Chamber of Commerce, Herts Business Incubator, Herts Business School, Herts Local Enterprise Partnership ("LEP"), Federation of Small Business, the University of Hertfordshire amongst others (Chartered Association of Business Schools, 2016; Department for Business, Energy & Industrial Strategy, 2018). Hertfordshire's external stakeholders play a key role in maturing local businesses, by facilitating the transfer of knowledge, by advocating for the efficient use of technology or by coaching entrepreneurs (Bischoff et al., 2017), persuasively expressing invested interest in ensuring the local economy flourishes through the growth and development of entrepreneurship (University of Hertfordshire, 2015).

By using visual indicators as in figure 2, it eases the method of identifying potential linkages between the entities forming the local business ecosystem. Establishing ties between entities enables the researcher to set out which body interacts most with the local businesses. Establishing

13

linkages will also show which external stakeholder interacts the most with micro and small businesses. This method of assessing external stakeholders' efficiency is introduced by the Systems Theory (Skyttner, 2001) which suggests that by making the above interpretations the researcher will identify the entity, also called the "node", which represents the centre of the business ecosystem. The Systems Theory defines the centre of the ecosystem as the node which interacts the most with all other nodes.

THEORETICAL FRAMEWORKS

The structure of the local business ecosystem is partially reflected through several academic theoretical frameworks which support explaining how the business community members interact between themselves and whether there are any power relations or patterns of engagements.

1. Stakeholder theory helps understand the balance of impact, interaction and influences which take place within the local ecosystem;

2. Systems theory outlines patterns and dependencies, explaining the dynamics and relationships which occur within an ecosystem;

3. Institutional theory helps understand whether there are any established processes within the business ecosystem which provide an element of advantage to an external stakeholder.

The next section will detail each theoretical framework and establish whether they can contribute to HBS' objective of becoming central to the local business community.

STAKEHOLDER THEORY

Stakeholder Theory is often employed in a business context, and it refers to groups of individuals or entities who can excerpt influence over the performance of an organisation on which they have invested interest for its production (Freeman, 2010). Stakeholder Theory is an appropriate model to use when analysing Hertfordshire's business ecosystem, as local

14

external stakeholder institutions from within the county such as Chamber of Commerce, Federation of Small Business ("FSB") and HBS have invested interest within the local economy and the way businesses perform (Brown, 2018). Bischoff et al., (2017) outline that a long-term inter-stakeholder relationship supporting the maturity and the creation of efficiencies within a business ecosystem will support business growth through their life cycle from formation to maturity.

When transposed to the context of this research, the Stakeholder Theory suggests these external institutions play a crucial role in enabling local micro and small firms to mature, by facilitating the transfer of business knowledge, by advising on efficient use of technology and by mentoring entrepreneurs (Chartered Association of Business Schools, 2016; Department for Business, Energy & Industrial Strategy, 2018; Bischoff, Volkmann and Audretsch, 2017). Freeman et al. (2014) emphasises the importance of collaboration and having a continuous partnership between all key stakeholder groups. However, the literature reviewed did not provide information as to who maintains this coordination within Hertfordshire between all its stakeholders bearing interest in the development of local small and micro firms.

Industry reports describe the existing entrepreneurial, micro and small ecosystem as organic and imperfect, being in a constant state of flux, either by utilising existing relationships or by creating new linkages, changing as necessary either to improve, to expand or to adjust to market conditions, while exchanging information with external stakeholders (Pitelis, 2012; Startup Genome Project, 2012; World Economic Forum, 2013). The Stakeholder Theory (Freeman, 2010) aligns itself with HBS' intention of becoming central to the local business community. However, to do so, the school must step in and stimulate to increase the number of interactions between itself, other external stakeholders and start-ups, particularly small businesses. This effect amplified throughout time will eventually provide the adequate credentials to HBS in the eyes of small businesses and start-ups, as far as the Stakeholder Theory suggests, and will enable its transition to the centre of the community (Spekman, Wittmannrt and Lambe, 2008).

Industry papers reveal their perception about the relationship between HBS and the other external local stakeholders as being driven by non-commercial incentives such as the business school offering access to premises, human capital and consultancy skills, in exchange for networking opportunities and reputational value (Chartered Association of Business Schools, 2016). There is evidence that indicates that entrepreneurial communities which are supported by business schools and universities (Audretsch et al., 2011; Dubini, 1989; Feldman et al., 2005; Wolfe, 2005), are advocating for up to 10 cultural, social, and material non-commercial attributes that ultimately return them benefits, including stimulating start-ups to interact and create relationships with other external stakeholders (University of Edinburgh Business School, 2017). These attributes include establishing a supporting culture (Aoyama, 2009; Feldman, 2001; Julien, 2007), training and nurturing talent (Arruda et al., 2014; Audretsch et al., 2011), encouraging networking (Dubini, 1989; Malecki, 1997; Neck et al., 2004), providing mentorship and role models (Feld, 2012; Kenney et al., 2005; World Economic Forum, 2013) and suggest Hertfordshire micro and small businesses could be absorbing influence from other local external stakeholders.

SYSTEMS THEORY

Existing literature looks at Hertfordshire's micro and small business and draws on the notion of the Systems Theory, whereby several entities also called "nodes" are creating local interactions between themselves forming a network of engagements having the shape of a mash (Miller et al., 2019). This academic theory is relevant for the Hertfordshire business ecosystem as it describes the patterns in which engagements are being formed between businesses and various external stakeholders, triggered by influence excerpted by the latter on the former (Lima, 2017). Despite these engagements being triggered based on local patterns and dependencies expressed mainly by businesses and satisfied by established support organisations, the literature does not provide information as to whether there is any coordination in these patterns. Moreover, the Systems Theory does not perceive any hierarchy between the member nodes (Skyttner, 2008), suggesting that engagements can happen at any time between them (Bakhtiar Rana and Allen, 2018). Given the theory does not explain what defines the hierarchy of the relationships in the centre and what factors drive a stakeholder to be in its centre, further research is necessary to establish the particularities and the complexities of Hertfordshire business ecosystem to uncover those within its specific context.

Marmol et al., 2015 find that inner-stakeholder relationships occur in various patterns and not only between businesses and institutions but also between two members of the business community and from different sectors. For example, an organisation from the tech industry getting commercial advice from a micro business in the professional services industry. The existing gap in literature specific to the coordination of these nodes which are interacting forming engagements (Miller et al., 2019) can potentially be closed by HBS which seeks to transition and become central to the Hertfordshire business ecosystem.

INSTITUTIONAL THEORY

Existing literature also looks at the Institutional Theory which complements the Stakeholder Theory by suggesting that business schools may excerpt a more powerful influence over the local micro and small businesses, compared to the market or economic pressures (Peters, 2010; Tihanyi et al., 2012) due to the perception they provide to the business community. Berthod (2018) highlights that organisations do not operate in a vacuum. Therefore, while seeking to explore new sources of knowledge to increase efficiencies in their internal processes, they may get exposed to external influences such as those provided by academic institutions and business schools. A direct correlation was drawn between the level of control HBS excerpts over local start-ups, micro and small businesses (Van der Borgh et al., 2012); however, further research is required to establish what indicators are to be used to enable the business school to measure the effectiveness of its influence.

In terms of paradoxes, Foreman (2019) shows the local business ecosystem is built on the back of Chaos vs Control paradox where on one end entities are interacting independently between themselves and on the other end there is a complete and controlled structured approach in place regulating each engagement between large established external stakeholders

(Schwartz-Salant, 2017). The theories identified above contribute by attempting to explain how the business community members interact between themselves. However, more research is required to understand the patterns and the peculiarities of the relationships formed within Hertfordshire business community (Ben Letaifa et al., 2013) to be able to advise HBS accordingly and pave the way for a successful transition.

TYPES OF ENGAGEMENTS

Although the literature reviewed does not provide a structured list of channels indicating which entity engages with which, two main patterns of interactions were identified, which involve business schools. Given the scope of the research project is to advise HBS on how to transition to a central role within its local business community, it is necessary to investigate these two types of engagements to enable the institution to maximise its value through them.

1. Engagements between external stakeholders (which includes HBS, UH) and local businesses

2. Engagements between UH or HBS, and local students

The following section will analyse each type of interaction and establish whether they generate any impact at the business community level.

EXTERNAL STAKEHOLDERS AND BUSINESSES

The Stakeholder Theory emphasises the importance of having embedded stakeholder relationships within the entrepreneurial ecosystem (Volkmann et al., 2017). The forms of mentorship found most efficient in existing theories for coaching entrepreneurs involve external stakeholders sharing experiences through lecturing and storytelling, through social events or networking opportunities (Bischoff et al., 2017). Literature review shows micro-businesses are faced with time pressures and staff shortages, while at the same time universities are subjected to high levels of competitiveness, therefore facilitating additional engagements between them brings its complexities and may raise barriers for both parties (Network, 2019; Forbes.com, 2018). In the context of this research paper,

18

it is essential that HBS, as an external stakeholder, establishes only active engagements which bring mutual benefits to both organisations but also the business school and university while enabling its transition to the centre of the business community.

Bischoff et al. (2017) reveal the role of external stakeholders is to transmit practical, real-life events and to outline to their audience formed from entrepreneurs and business owners, the lessons learnt and takeaways from each scenario are enriching their experiences, allowing conversations to follow. In the context of this research project, this can be achieved both ways by exposing small businesses to academic advice and by exposing academic staff to real challenges encountered by companies to enrich the academic curriculum. This process generates a power dynamic between companies and the university where each party has both an invested interest but also the duty to contribute with information to enable the interaction to take place. This paper requires further research to establish whether HBS leverages this power dynamic in its transition to the heart of the local business ecosystem. In terms of the content of mentorship programmes, one can challenge the relevancy, and the generalisability of the substance taught within an academic environment and whether it can uniformly satisfy all local businesses or whether variations must be added based on industries, sectors or business maturity levels (Management Learning, 2014). The above observations warrant further research conducted in the context of HBS to establish if the institution considers mentoring entrepreneurs. If it does, additional research is required to determine what niche HBS has prioritised and whether it uses this strategy to add value and enable the transition towards the core of the Herts business community.

STUDENTS AND LOCAL BUSINESSES

Industry papers provide examples of partnership initiatives conducted by 40 UK universities, business schools and local businesses where students are given the option to enrol in apprenticeship programmes involving both academic teaching and industry placement. By engaging with the industry during their educational programme, students will gain exposure to real-life challenges and well-practised methodologies used for problem-solving within commercial contexts (Chartered Association of Business Schools, 2016). Paton et al. (2014) argue that these hybrid teaching initiatives generate mutual benefits for both students and micro and small businesses, effectively enriching the local economy with a future workforce capable of hitting the ground running and deliver excellent results immediately after graduation. The literature reviewed does inform that UH included within its portfolio of courses several apprenticeship degrees. However, it does not clarify whether the decision to include these courses was made to enable the academic institution to increase its linkages with local businesses, to add value to the local business ecosystem and in doing so aim to shift to a central role within the Hertfordshire business community.

BUSINESS ECOSYSTEM CHALLENGES

While interpreting the academic theories identified to be relevant, associated with Herts' business ecosystem and HBS' intention to transition to the heart of its local business community, several challenges have emerged. These challenges require investigating to establish whether they pose any threats to the desired outcome of HBS' transition or to the rollout of its target business model, which will be advised through this research project. The next section investigates each challenge by consulting existing literature.

MANAGEMENT OF EXTERNAL STAKEHOLDERS

Wilson (2012) sets out the need to have a thorough understanding of all external stakeholders including their capabilities to coordinate and optimise collaboration across the ecosystem and achieve effective linkages between the right entities at the right time.

Despite having an essential role in the development of local businesses (Bischoff et al., 2017), the literature reviewed did not reveal a formal managerial process such as a centralised relational map, to capture all external stakeholders' interactions with local businesses or capabilities provided by the former and accessed by the latter (Miller et al., 2019). Limited information was provided by several external stakeholders (University of Hertfordshire 2, 2018; Biopark.co.uk, 2018; Chambers, 2019), however, according to the Stakeholder's Theory, a thorough investigation is necessary to fully understand the stakeholders' objectives and limitations for local businesses (Skyttner, 2006).

TRANSFORMATION JOURNEY

Existing literature highlights that large support institutions are excerpting influence over micro and small businesses to structure themselves efficiently and to set up and transition using effective business models (Carayannis et al., 2016; Provence et al., 2011; Carayannis et al., 2018). However, the literature review identified a gap around the implications of a business model transformation for business schools (Cavalcante et al., 2011). This research project will investigate these implications while establishing how the academic institution should transition to a more central role, using a fit for purpose business model (Teece, 2010).

CENTRAL GOVERNMENT STEER

Although the general direction is provided from the central government in the form of policies (Hertfordshire County Council, 2018), the literature reviewed revealed no single point of contact appointed from Westminster to manage the relationships between local businesses and the external stakeholders in Hertfordshire. However, industry papers reveal information about Hertfordshire Local Enterprise Partnership ("Hertfordshire LEP") working closely with the central government. Evidence also shows LEP is managing a £265 million, 6-year long investment programme designed to develop smaller local projects such as Growth Hub, The Careers & Enterprise Company and Enterprise Zone, ultimately to provide support and funding to micro and small local businesses (SemLEP, 2019). Hertfordshire Local Council is another institution partially funded from central government which tailored their online presence to create linkages and offer support to firms in the context of trading standards, mediation through ombudsman services, and additional local visibility through the use of business directories (Hertfordshire Local Council, 2019).

Steer from the central government is captured by various smaller institutions and converted into best practice technical notes circulated within the internet, encouraging entrepreneurship and aiming to socialise

21

concepts such as entrepreneurship education and linkages between learning providers micro and small businesses (The Quality Assurance Agency, 2018). Several independent groups and small organisations have gathered, centralised on a single page and published structured information about grants and loans including those created through incentives from central government, offering entrepreneurs an organised catalogue of resources (Entrepreneur Handbook, 2019). However, the literature reviewed very little information about HBS and whether the business school has close connections with the central government or any of its agencies or whether it plans to leverage on potential new linkages as part of its initiative to transition to the core of the local business community.

THE EFFECTS OF THE CHALLENGES

The above unknowns are generating a less than harmonious collaboration and weaker linkages as described by the Systems Theory and lack of transparency within the local business ecosystem (Miller et al., 2019). Further research is necessary to establish whether a business model transformation can address them by providing access to business knowledge, innovation and academic steer (Chartered Association of Business Schools, 2016).

HIGHER EDUCATION INSTITUTIONS

Department for Education (2017) states that the population of Hertfordshire has a higher proportion of qualifications of 42% than the national average of 37% and is expressing a higher level of interest in education, therefore creating a competitive environment for learning providers.

Hamilton (2016) writes that in addition to the academic research and teaching activities, a new opportunity was introduced for educational institutions to undertake an interfacing role between local businesses and their academic subject matter experts ("SME"). In doing so, the learning providers will create local partnerships and embed themselves in local projects, bridging the gap between small firms and academia while enacting two-way support relationships designed to exchange academic knowledge with real-life experience and challenges (Collinson, 2017).

22

Audretsch et al. (2011) highlight that the effects of putting this opportunity in practice will transform business schools into central hubs of knowledge and steer which will enable microbusinesses, particularly start-ups to have a stable growth by providing them with business knowledge and incentive for innovation.

Existing literature acknowledges that having business schools in the centre of their local business ecosystems will also create connections between a large number of micro-businesses and the smaller number of medium and large organisations making information exchange more efficient, opening up opportunities particularly for entrepreneurs (Blackburn, 2017). Owning this information, we can now re-arrange figure 2 from section external stakeholders into figure 20 and begin to consider what Herts' business ecosystem will look like, particularly what the linkages between its external stakeholders if HBS would occupy its centre.

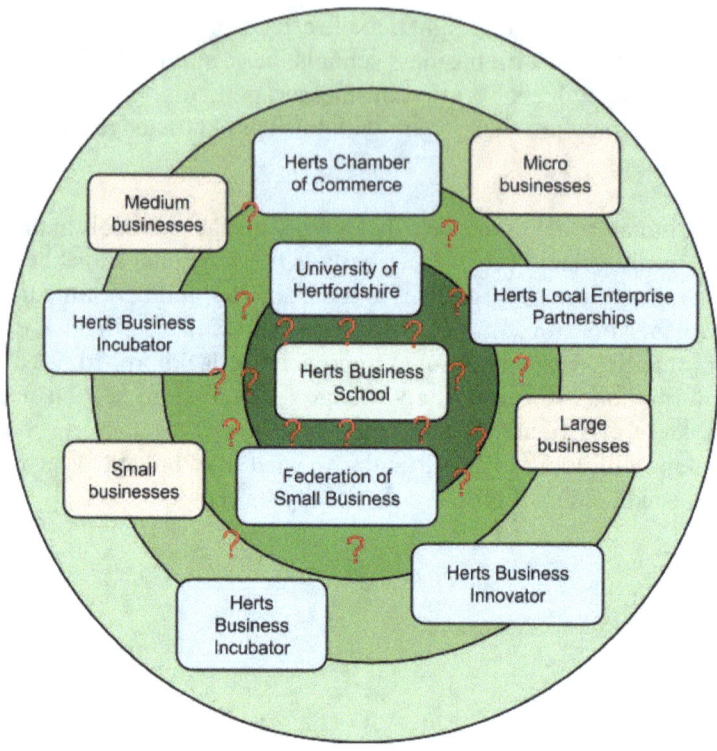

Figure 20: Herts' local business ecosystem having HBS in its centre

Existing literature encourages universities and other higher education institutions to undertake mentoring roles in training entrepreneurs and supporting micro-businesses from their local business communities (Dubini, 1989; Feldman et al., 2005; Wolfe, 2005). Chartered Association of Business Schools (2018) goes further by encouraging learning providers to create long term engagement interfaces and delegate existing academic staff to engage with their local industries. CABS advice also recommends for the creation of forums to transfer insights between members from their local business communities, while Kuratko (2005) encourages universities to diverse their curriculums with entrepreneurship courses informed from industry real business scenarios.

Existing literature does provide a vast catalogue of generic external stakeholders which can potentially influence local firms by enabling collaboration and informing entrepreneurship education, as shown in figure 3 (Bischoff et al., 2017; Hertfordshire Local Council, 2019; Hertfordshire LEP, 2019; Fayolle, 2018). However, there is no similar map or similar visual perspective created for Hertfordshire's business community, should HBS be positioned in its centre.

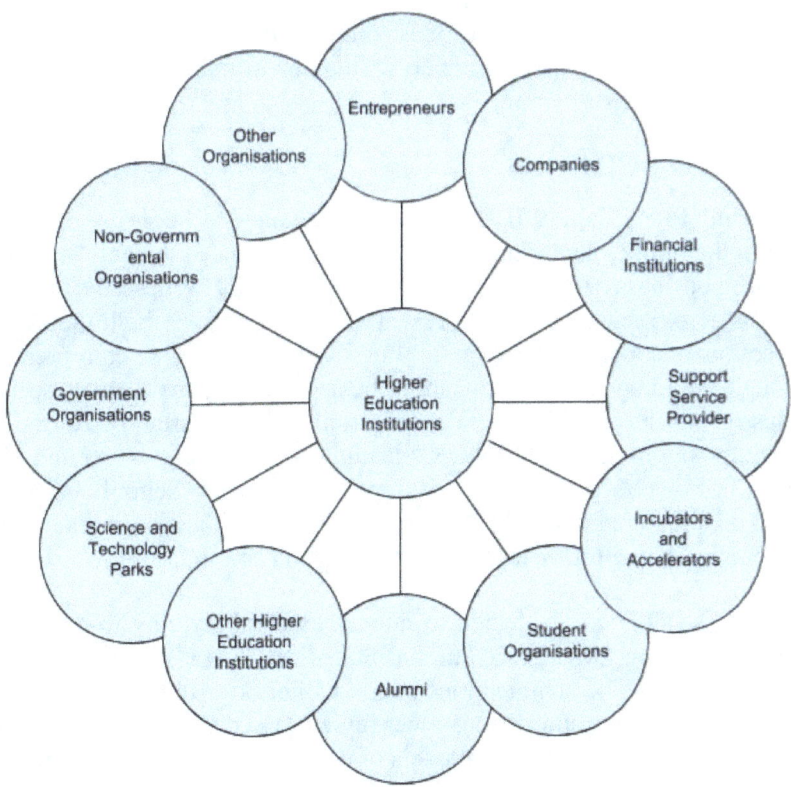

Figure 3: External stakeholder groups engaging with HE institutions

By considering the case of Herts' business community, the research project seeks to understand the nature of its local relationships while particularising the above theoretical model (Marmol et al., 2015). Also, it

25

aims to take into consideration other external influences such as higher competition between local learning providers (The Economist, 2018), variations in the national interest in undertaking higher education (Wedge et al., 2009), limitations in government funding (BBC News, 2019), general concerns about graduates' employability and readiness levels (Helyer et al., 2014) and others. It is noted that the incentives found within the literature for higher education institutions to secure the central role of their local business communities, mainly refer to their local business school (Chartered Association of Business Schools, 2018) therefore the next section of this paper will analyse this opportunity from the business schools' perspective.

BUSINESS SCHOOLS

According to Yazdani (2012), over 12,000 business schools are operating across the globe, and one in seven undergraduate students are now studying business or a related subject. Ivory et al. (2018) describe business schools across the UK as being essential contributors for both the British economy, but also in developing future consultants and entrepreneurs through the integration of education, business engagement and research. Industry papers provide confidence, despite the uncertainty caused by Brexit, positioning one of the UK's leading business schools second after one of France's within the European Business School Rankings (Rankings.ft.com, 2018) which suggests business schools have maintained a strong influence for their local economies and communities.

Business schools are subjected to intense external scrutiny from various bodies including Office for National Statistics ("ONS"), Department for Education ("DE"), Universities and Colleges Admissions Service ("UCAS"), Unistats and various other review-based comparison websites. Bernard (2012) finds that high levels of scrutiny are likely to obstruct the rollout of change programmes and goes further by saying that amending a business school's business model is deemed to be a rather long-term transformation process, which is likely to be frustrated by various regulatory barriers. Dennin (2019) emphasises that high levels of scrutiny, regulation combined with competitivity may even act as a deterrent, discouraging business transformation within an academic environment.

However, establishing the actual regulatory impact in the context of business transformation requires further research specific to HBS. Yazdani (2012) defines three types of business schools if measured based on their business models[3], their approach to knowledge sharing and the structure of their curriculum, as shown in figure 4:

1. The research focused business schools primarily focused on having a top-class research agenda, which have embedded characteristics of their previous clients and institutional heritage embedded within their cultures;
2. Teaching focused business schools concerned with the excellence character in teaching and the learning experience offered to their students, integrating modern and flexible teaching techniques;
3. Integration focused business schools concentrated on the interactions and the exchange of information with local firms who are providing analytical and reporting business insights for academic research and also informing and updating the teaching and learning experience by advising on emerging industry needs.

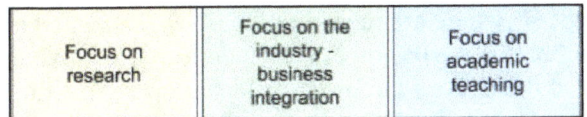

Figure 4: Business school types based on their priorities

Mason (2015) highlights each type of business school contributes to the local economy in a slightly different manner based on its contribution to the other external stakeholders and local businesses, who are forming the local business ecosystem. Denning (2014) states that if a business school is focused on research, it is likely to influence the local business ecosystem by providing scientists, a business school focused on academic teaching is expected to produce a highly academically educated workforce. Likewise,

---

[3] A business model is the catalogue of processes representative to an organisation which constitute fundamental aspects of it including scope, clientele or interactions with third parties, market offerings, strategies, structure, practices, operational processes, policies and other representative characteristics (Osterwalder and Pigneur, 2013)

a business school focused on business integration is likely to influence the local business community by providing highly skilled graduates with relevant work experience. The previously described academic trend which empowers business schools to secure a central role within their local business ecosystems (Fsb.org.uk, 2019) sets the foundation for HBS' objective to tailor its existing business model to reposition itself within Hertfordshire's business community. However, in doing so, it is necessary first to establish the current business model operated by HBS (Tuccillo, 2002). After determining the current condition, the research project must outline the capabilities specific to Herts business community, that HBS should demonstrate, so that is accepted by other external stakeholders including micro and small local businesses (Department for Education, 2017) as their new central point (Deloitte, 2019; Chartered Association of Business Schools, 2016). Further research is necessary to establish the current condition and which type of business model is likely to serve best HBS and enable it to transition and become central to the local business community.

Another factor that shapes the academic institution's business models consists of the way they are ranked (WU, 2019; Top Universities, 2019). Business schools, as well as other academic learning providers, are being formally rated through a centralised national portal which measures each entity based on several universally applicable pre-set key performance indicators ("KPIs") (London, 1995). For each KPI, students are invited to provide grades, during and after the course of the academic programme (Unistats.ac.uk, 2018). The feedback is focused on the student experience, perceived through the eyes of the student. Therefore, the approach is criticised about the subjectivity of the questions students are asked to respond to (Mansfield, 2000). The current KPIs are based on student satisfaction and continuation of studies. However, they do not measure the level of integration within the industry demonstrated throughout the duration of the academic studies (Unistats.ac.uk, 2018) which means as far as the national ranking systems for educational learning providers is concerned, industry integration and the formation of linkages with other external stakeholders is not a priority during the education years. However, national post-graduation surveys tailored their questionnaires to enquire former students about the level of employment and embeddedness within the industry reached after six months, three years respectively, from their graduation dates (Unistats.ac.uk, 2018). In doing so, Unistats have shifted the focus of scrutiny from initially assessing the study period only to evaluating the post-study period, which includes graduates' readiness for industry integration. Smerdon et al. (2018) provided that the latter is influenced directly by the level of industry exposure experienced by students while being in education.

Hooley et al. (2013) highlight that Unistats as well as other benchmarking platforms that rank business schools should no longer only rely on internal factors but should also measure the institution's effectiveness while considering their impact on the local business communities. Marmol et al. (2015) emphasise that it becomes inevitable to consider external factors such as collaboration with local firms embedded within the academic curriculum when ranking educational learning providers, which aligns with HBS' long term plans of securing a central role within its local business ecosystem.

EARLY ALIGNMENT WITH THE INDUSTRY

Kruss (2006) highlights that the new academic benchmarking trend decreases slightly with the historical focus set only on the quality of research and teaching and emphasises on setting up a new alignment between students and the industries, by exposing them to business insights, business challenges and problem-solving processes. However, it can be argued that this new measuring trend excerpts pressures on the academic institutions to change their business models to adjust their outputs, i.e. curriculum profile and transferable skills (Universities UK, 2016). Miller et al. (2019) encourage a more formalised collaboration between universities and businesses, allowing for inter ecosystem relationships which aim to nurture the concept of entrepreneurship education and improve employability rates. However, existing literature does not provide a method to quantify the level of industry embeddedness necessary for further research to establish a bespoke business model suitable for BHS and its local business community, starting from existing examples documented by other business schools across the UK (Chartered Association of Business Schools, 2018).

Despite the vast amount of literature describing the three different types of business models identified in figure 4, including their contribution to the local business ecosystems and shortfalls, there is no literature presenting a transformation journey from one model to another (Cornuel, 2005). When the dynamics of the business ecosystem change the demand expressed by business communities, local stakeholders including business schools must also adjust their offerings to suit the new market, protect the integrity of their existing linkages and their position within the ecosystem and remain sustainable (Karhiniemi, 2009). For example, if a business school focused on research with only 10% of their time spent on local community engagement is subjected to external factors which dictate the new focus should be to engage with external stakeholders at least 40% of their time. The business school is to adjust its business model to allow for an increase in community engagement of at least 30% of their time (Lorange et al., 2014). Although business change and transformation are well documented in general, the literature reviewed provided no evidence of journals or industry papers to support the business model transformation for a large well-established academic institution or business school.

Also, the reviewed literature does not provide correlations between any of the three types of business schools the business model highlighted in figure 4 and a potential central position within the local business community. This information suggests each local business ecosystem may prefer a particular type of business school in its proximity (Department for Education, 2017; Department for Communities and Local Government, 2015). Therefore, it will require further research to establish what necessities Herts' business ecosystem has and what business model HBS should embrace to address them (UK Commission for Employment and Skills, 2014).

HERTFORDSHIRE BUSINESS SCHOOL

HBS is categorised about Hertfordshire business ecosystem as an external stakeholder, with an invested interest in the local business community, seeking to facilitate up to a specific extent linkage between businesses and both academic staff and students through various educational programmes. HBS' aims to secure the middle seat within Hertfordshire's business ecosystem (Cornuel, 2005) and so a gap is acknowledged between its current state and business model, and the condition it seeks to reach in the future and a fit for purpose target business model (Osterwalder et al., 2013). Chartered Association of Business Schools (2016) provides examples of programmes and initiatives carried out by HBS seeking to help social entrepreneurs facing growth challenges associated with micros and small firms, such as lack of resources and operational inefficiencies. Also, industry papers provide information about activities conducted by HBS as early as 2007, to promote innovation in marketing, product development and operational matters while introducing funding schemes to wave consultancy costs (Chartered Association of Business Schools, 2016). Despite revealing some evidence of engagement with the broader business community such as the above and the Chartered Manager Degree Apprenticeship ("CMDA") strategic partnership (Department for Education, 2017), the literature reviewed does not provide an exhaustive list of initiatives carried out by HBS making it challenging to establish whether the institution's efforts are sufficient or otherwise to enable them to secure a central role.

CONCLUSION

Existing literature generally perceives UK business schools as high profile influential institutions with robust credentials and the authority to improve the local economy by providing students with quality education and early exposure to industry work experience. Academic trends do encourage the formation of interaction between business schools and local businesses by highlighting the advantages of combining theoretical knowledge with real-life industry challenges. However, in the case of HBS, the literature reviewed provided only a partial map of relationships between itself and other stakeholders from Hertfordshire business ecosystem shown in figure 2 from this paper's section: external stakeholders, making it difficult to weight each linkage and establish who may be considered central to the local business community. Also, very little information was revealed about HBS' business model, making it necessary to conduct further research before establishing how a business model transformation is to be delivered to enable HBS to be more central to its local business ecosystem.

Existing theoretical frameworks define the concepts of external stakeholders, which are attributed to local organisations and authorities which are also engaging with local businesses. However, the literature does not describe the relationship between these stakeholders through theory, nor does it define who undertakes the coordination duty of those entities to ensure harmonious communication and the consistency of interactions. Further research is required to advise HBS on how it can tailor its business model, to reposition itself at the core of Hertfordshire business ecosystem. The next steps are to fill in the gaps identified in the literature review and establish facts in the following themes:

1. Define the stakeholders who are forming the Hertfordshire business ecosystem and map the relationships between them, including those involving HBS;

2. Understand HBS' existing operating priorities and how it contributes and maintains relationships with other business community stakeholders;

3. Explore any "missed opportunities" in terms of relationships and linkages which could position HBS in the heart of the local business community;

4. Suggest a strategy that will transform HBS' business model to enable it to capitalise on additional opportunities and support its transition to the core of the local business ecosystem.

The next chapter will explain the methods of data collection and their analysis and justify their appropriateness to achieve the research objectives.

RESEARCH METHODOLOGY

INTRODUCTION

In line with the conceptual framework constructed through the literature and reflected in figure 2 from the section: external stakeholders, this paper adopts a qualitative exploratory approach (Stebbins, 2001), using Hertfordshire business ecosystem in a single case study method. This method is appropriate as it accounts for the peculiarities of both the Hertfordshire business ecosystem and the business model of HBS. Also, it allows an in-depth exploration of the objectives and addresses the research aim theoretically - by enriching the theoretical model, but also practically - by deriving practical recommendations for a specific business school.

RESEARCH OBJECTIVES

The following four research objectives were first identified in the section: CONCLUSIONS and are aimed to address the literature review gaps and fulfil the underlying project scope.

Research objective 1: Understanding the local business ecosystem including the parties involved and the interactions between them

The literature reviewed has indicated the existence of a local business ecosystem and appointed several stakeholder institutions, as shown in figure 2 from the EXTERNAL STAKEHOLDERS section. However, at a theoretical level, the entities forming the business ecosystem in the subject are perceived to interact in a non-coordinated fashion. Also, the literature reviewed provided no well-defined mechanism to measure the level of engagement between the entities, making it unclear which stakeholder is likely to have secured a central role around which local businesses revolve. This complexity is going to be resolved by researching and constructing a comprehensive map which shows all the relationships involving all stakeholders and members of the local business community.

Research objective 2: Understanding HBS' potential contribution to the local business ecosystem

While attempting to understand the nature of the linkages which take place within the local business ecosystem which include HBS, several relevant theories have been identified (see section THEORETICAL FRAMEWORKS) including the provision of general incentives for collaboration and involvement of industry representatives, students and academic staff, through many educational programmes.

Research objective 3: Exploring missed opportunities in terms of relationships with other stakeholders

Several industry papers provide examples of other business schools actively pursuing to create linkages with micro and small businesses from their regions of the UK. The research will establish the extent to which HBS can re-model its operations and potentially add new roles and responsibilities which HBS could undertake, to address the primary needs expressed by its local business community.

Research objective 4: Explore strategies that will transform HBS' business model to a more central position for the local business community

It is recognised that a business model transformation may be required for HBS, to reposition itself in the heart of a local business community. However, given that there are no prescribed guidelines at the theoretical level towards business model change in the higher education sector, the investigation will focus on the current priorities of HBS established within Herts' business ecosystem climate.

RESEARCH METHODS OF DATA COLLECTION

The nature of the objectives makes it necessary to use both primary and secondary research methods to establish complete information and to advise accordingly using the methodology indicated by the Research Onion research model reflected in figure 5 (Saunders et al., 2012). The primary research method aims to capture various perspectives from different leaders of external stakeholder institutions and organisations through semi-structured interviews about the local business ecosystem. Secondary research aims to consolidate and verify the findings with data

34

obtained from industry papers, local council reports and official statistics, having the overall objective to construct a broader comprehensive picture of the business ecosystem, while identifying what characteristics must a central point demonstrate and how should HBS transition to that position.

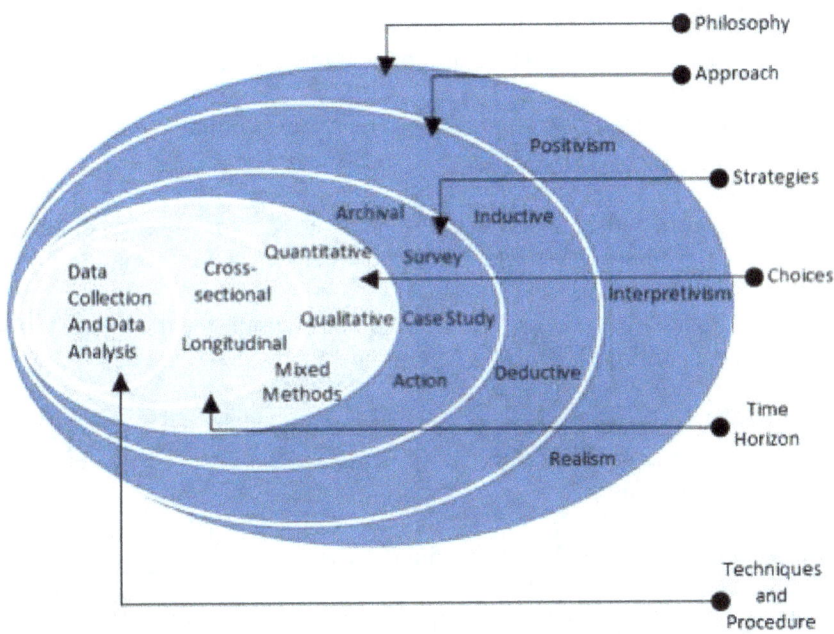

Figure 5: Research Onion (Saunders et al., 2012)

SEMI-STRUCTURED INTERVIEWS

A series of semi-structured, 45 to 60 minutes, 1-2-1 interviews will be scheduled with leaders of various external stakeholders of the Hertfordshire external business ecosystem, as highlighted in figure 20 from section HIGHER EDUCATION INSTITUTIONS, to understand their perception of the four research questions and set the foundation for secondary research. Alternative methods have been considered, such as focus groups or surveys. However, the comprehensiveness of the information sought from the interviewees and the particularities of each response warranted that to facilitate thorough qualitative research, and semi-structured interviews are the only suitable method. The meetings will be conducted using a top-down approach which will touch on the following themes:

1. Establish the structure of the local business ecosystem;

2. Identify the linkages between the nodes within the ecosystem, as defined by the systems theory (Bertalanffy, 2015);

3. Identify the stakeholders' contributions to entrepreneurs and micro-businesses, including dependencies and information flows;

4. Identify where HBS and UH are within the ecosystem and concerning the business community;

5. Identify what changes must be achieved by HBS and UH to reposition themselves more centrally within the local business community.

The theoretical sample, i.e. the candidates for the interviews (listed in table 1) were selected based on the findings from the literature reviewed, which indicated a list of potential external stakeholders who influence the local business community through their actions or services.

The visual representation of the theoretical sample is reflected on the ecosystem visual map, in figure 2 from the external stakeholders' section. The speculative sample was selected in such a way to represent both UH perspectives equally but also opinions constructed independently of UH.

The aim of having both internal and external to UH interviewees is to maintain impartiality for University of Hertfordshire's involvement within the local business community.

STAKEHOLDER INSTITUTION	ROLE OF THE INTERVIEWEE
University of Hertfordshire Business School	
University of Hertfordshire Business School	
University of Hertfordshire Business Incubator	Executive leader or associate
Hertfordshire LEP	
Hertfordshire Chamber of Commerce	
East of England Federation of Small Businesses	

Primary research - list of interviewees

COUNCIL REPORTS AND FORMAL STATISTICS

Secondary research methods are employed to verify and complement the information provided during the primary research stage and draw relevant conclusions around the consistency, or otherwise, of findings. Secondary research also aims to remove any ambiguity resulted from primary research and allows accurate conclusions to be drawn on the four research objectives. The following sources are set to be used for secondary research: industry papers, local council reports and formal statistics released by the Office of National Statistics (ONS, 2019).

DATA ANALYSIS

The data analysis process varies for each research objective and research method employed. The role of the primary research data analysis is to extract the main themes from the interview answers and create an initial map of characteristics which will later inform the secondary research. Thematic study on interview records will be conducted to extract and interpret commonalities and differences between the complex principal questions. It is appropriate to use a thematic analysis as it enables pinpointing and recording patterns of themes which can be extracted and associated with the research questions.

The method of creating thematic analysis for this research project involves transcribing the interview recordings, identifying keywords, distinguishing the categories of keywords which are later converted into themes and finally associated with the research questions. Secondary data analysis was conducted by extracting data which was previously published on ONS (2019), public governmental catalogues and online search engines. This process is done by structuring them in themes and associating them with the results of the primary data research to understand the structure of the local business ecosystem.

It also cross-analyses the primary data to verify consistency and make recommendations to HBS to maximise the value for the local business ecosystem.

DATA VALIDITY AND RELIABILITY

Although Yin (2008) argues that single method studies are not as complicated as hybrid methods, care must be applied when rationalising primary and secondary research data, to uniformise the information and achieve a reliable analysis. The process of triangulation through the combination of primary and secondary research (Ridenour et al., 2008) will mitigate potential biases arising from the author's interpretation of the interview's responses.

Primary research will be conducted with six interviewees, three from which are working under the UH umbrella, with the other three employed by other external organisations. This process is also a form of triangulation and is taken to avoid ambiguity and maintain impartiality in terms of the answers concerning the university's involvement within the local business ecosystem.

Another limitation consists of differences in the volume of knowledge and expertise held by the interview participants about the business ecosystem, reflected in a significant difference between the amount of data provided by one interviewee compared to another.

LIMITATIONS ARISING FROM THE METHODOLOGY

One limitation is the small number of interviewees (six) compared to the size of the Hertfordshire business ecosystem and the necessity to maintain a qualitative research approach. This means that a less demanding method such as an online survey would have produced less substance but perhaps would have allowed reaching out to more representatives from the local business community. However, given the need to conduct interviews to maintain the quality and depth of data received, it would be advisable for future research to allocate additional resources to reach out to more representatives of the business community.

RISK AND QUALITY MANAGEMENT

The interviews are audio-recorded and will be stored on HBS' cloud infrastructure as per UH Ethics Committee terms and conditions. The approach will make possible the verification of the primary research data, resulted from the theming procedure, whenever required.

The risks associated with neutrality and the researchers' impartiality for data collection, given the author of this project's affiliation with HBS (Crotty, 1998) will be managed throughout the entire research project by annexing evidence and by welcoming analysis from others for verification and audit. To avoid generic interpretation biases, although partially neutralised by the use of secondary research, the researcher of this paper will write at the end of the research project a reflective piece which will capture any signs of a bias influence and potential lack of impartiality. If at that stage, signs of any bias are detected, alternative data sources will be explored, and the researcher will request supervision support as appropriate (Pulla and Schissel, 2018).

The project's output is a business model designed to apply only to HBS, and in line with the number of external stakeholders interviewed, it should not be generalised and applied to other business schools, making generalisability a non-issue (Maxwell, 2009). However, the above does not mean that the project's output can never be generalised, nor that the method employed in achieving this output cannot be applied to a different institution. The qualitative nature of the project and its particulars are making it non-generalisable.

The next section will analyse primary and secondary research findings in line with the methodology outlined above.

DATA FINDINGS AND ANALYSIS

The insights obtained during primary research were analysed, rationalised and structured in several themes which will be outlined and interpreted in conjunction with secondary research, within the data analysis section. However, the insights obtained belong equally to functions within UH (University of Hertfordshire Business School, University of Hertfordshire Business Incubator), but also to three external stakeholders from the broader business community (Hertfordshire LEP, East of England Federation of Small Businesses). This balance maintains impartiality concerning HBS and its objectives of becoming central to the local business community.

THE SIZE OF THE BUSINESS ECOSYSTEM

The primary research revealed over 55 different entities influencing Hertfordshire's business ecosystem. This figure was obtained by adding up all distinct stakeholder entities referred to by interviewees when asked to list the parties which are changing Hertfordshire's business community. However, it is noted that some of the responses refer to collective entities such as "Networking Groups", "Supply Chain" and "Banks". Secondary research revealed over 50 distinct results when researching "Networking Groups" in Hertfordshire (STANTA, 2019; Ukcitynetworking.com, 2019). A thorough analysis of the primary research results identified at least 25% of the results as being collective entities. After combining both the primary and secondary research, when the collective bodies are outlined as individual legal entities, the number of stakeholders influencing the local business community expands to over 800 distinct legal entities and groups as shown in figure 6.

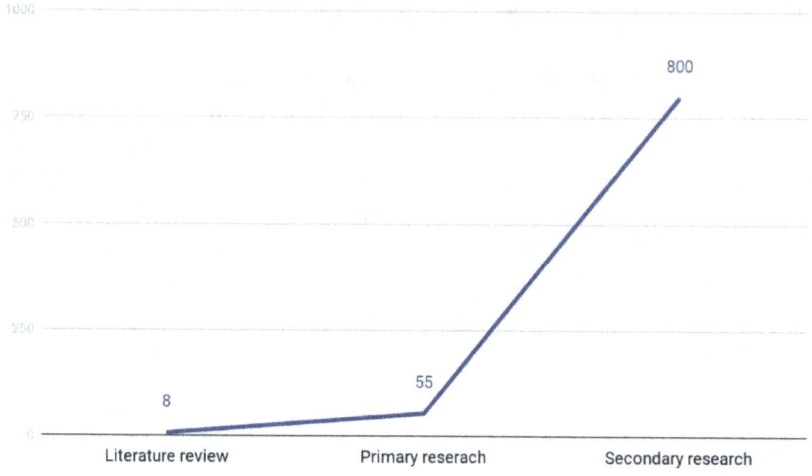

Figure 6: The size of the local business ecosystem

STAKEHOLDER RANKING

The primary research revealed 55 distinct entities mentioned during the course of the five interviews. The study investigates the frequency and contexts in which these entities are referred to establish a hierarchy between them. The objective also includes understanding which stakeholders contribute and influence most to the local business ecosystem. In doing so, the primary research found the following ten stakeholders as having the highest level of influence[4] over the business community.

---

[4] An external stakeholder's level of influence is calculated based on the number of references made by each interviewee about each external stakeholder

GRADED BASED ON THE
INTERVIEW MENTIONS

	Advice on Finance	Business Community	Dacorum Borough	Economic Development Teams	Exemplas	Federation of Small Business	Further Education Colleges	HBS	Hertfordshire Growth Hub	Hertfordshire LEP	Herts Chamber of Commerce	Innovation Vouchers	LEP
Party 2 - total mentions during all interviews													
Herts Chamber of Commerce		6			1	1			1				
Wenta		5	1			1			1				
Hertfordshire Growth Hub	1	5			1	1	1		1				
HBS		5				1				1	1		
Federation of Small Business		5						1					
Hertfordshire LEP		4				1							
Welwyn & Hatfield Chamber of Commerce		3			1	1							
UH		3				1							
Institute of Directors		3				1							

Figure 7: Most influential stakeholders (collective view from primary research based on the number of references)

However, a closer analysis of the similarities expressed by the interviewees shows there is minimal consensus about their priority. For example, although it had obtained the highest score, Herts Chamber of Commerce is not perceived as being the most influential entity by all interviews. Furthermore, the second external stakeholder (according to the collective ranking system) does not benefit from the same level of appreciation across all five interviewees, i.e. Wenta's rankings vary between position 1 (interviewee 4) and place 5 (interviewee 5).

Position in the collective ranking system	Position in the individual hierarchy				
	Int[6]. 1	Int. 2	Int. 3	Int. 4	Int. 5
(position no. 1) Herts Chamber of Commerce[7]	1[8]	9	8		
(position no. 2) Wenta		2		1	5
(position no. 3) Hertfordshire Growth Hub	9			2	2
(position no. 4) HBS					1
(position no. 5) Federation of Small Business	2				
(position no. 6) Hertfordshire LEP	8		9		
(position no. 7) Welwyn & Hatfield Chamber of Commerce		3		5	6
(position no. 8) UH	3	4			8
(position no. 9) Institute of Directors			5		

Figure 8: Most influential stakeholders (collective view from primary research based on the number of linkages)

TYPES OF STAKEHOLDERS

The types of stakeholders vary in many ways depending on the commercial objective, the service they provide, their position concerning businesses and their maturity level, as shown in figure 21. These can be commercial and seek a form of subscription (i.e. Federation of Small Businesses, Herts Chamber of Commerce) which have been categorised as membership organisations or non-commercial and offer services without having a financial expectation (i.e. Hertfordshire Growth Hub). In terms of the

---

[5] Int. = Interview participant number X
[6] Position within the collective ranking list
[7] Position within the interviewee's individual ranking

services stakeholders provide, they can enable networking opportunities (i.e. Institute of Directors, St Albans Business Network), provide support on a one-on-one basis (Exemplas, banks, Wenta) or offer a long-term group coaching which also opens up networking opportunities (i.e. UH Business Incubator).

External stakeholders can be focused solely on providing support to businesses at a particular stage of their life cycle (i.e. Hertfordshire LEP enabling large companies) or can focus on delivering a broad portfolio of services allowing firms to pick and choose what suits them best (i.e. Power, broadband services, banks). Another method of categorising stakeholders refers to the size of the average business requesting support, varying from start-ups and small businesses which are likely to be assisted by Herts Chamber of Commerce or Federation of Small Business. On the other end of the scale, Hertfordshire LEP is perceived as a local representative of the central government, known to be interpreting [direction from] Department of Business and Innovation Strategy and allocate funding of £20M. The regional coverage also makes the subject of another method by which local stakeholders are seen as either localised such as business advisors, more regional such as Federation of Small Business, Herts Chamber of Commerce or Hertfordshire Growth Club or Countrywide solution that need start-up advice such as Wenta.

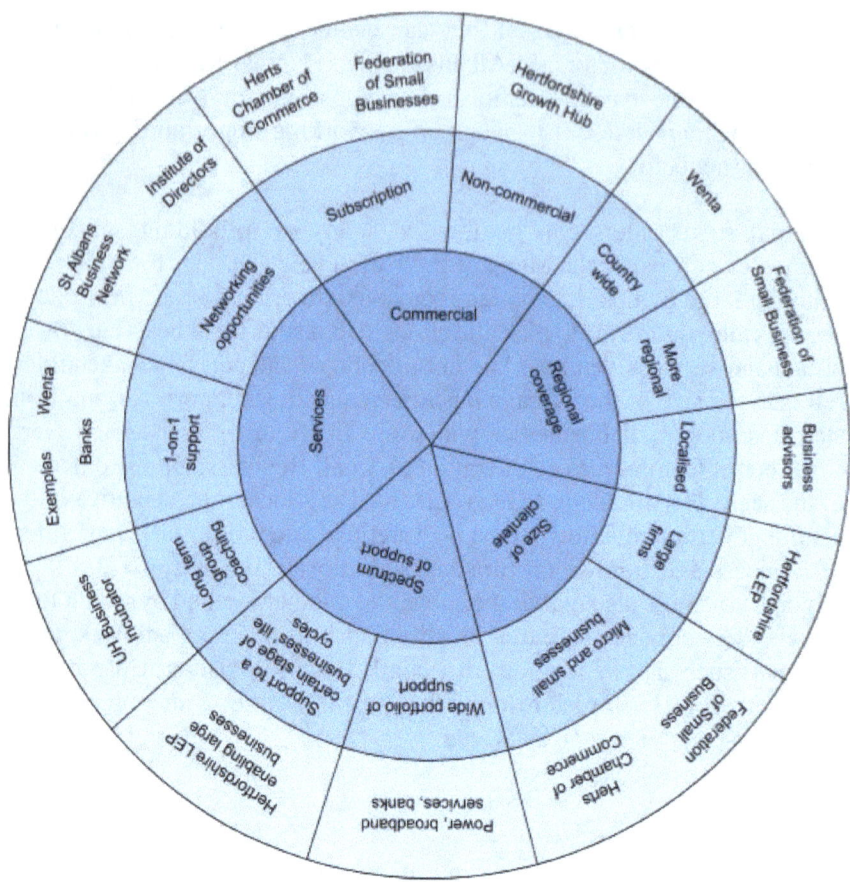

Figure 21: Herts' business ecosystem - methods of categorising external stakeholders

STAKEHOLDER RELATIONSHIPS

According to primary research, in terms of stakeholder to stakeholder interactions (therefore excluding local firms), Federation of Small Business engages the most with other external stakeholders. In terms of stakeholder to businesses engagements, Herts Chamber of Commerce appears to have the most influence according to primary research. However, secondary research revealed Wenta has the most significant contribution to local firms in terms of offering support (which scores second place in primary research), followed by Hertfordshire Growth Hub (which scores the 3rd place in primary research). The interactions between external stakeholders, if projected in a visual format using dots (representing stakeholders) and lines (representing the linkages between the former), would form the shape of a mash. If there were no prioritisation or filtering mechanism for the external stakeholders, the output would be a network of nodes similar to the one described in the Systems Theory (Skyttner, 2001) within section THEORETICAL FRAMEWORKS, represented in figure 9, made out of 55 entities influencing the local business community and 164 relationships between them, in line with initial research results. If secondary research results are employed the number of external stakeholders increases to ~800, and the number of linkages and relationships between them also increases exponentially to ~2,400.

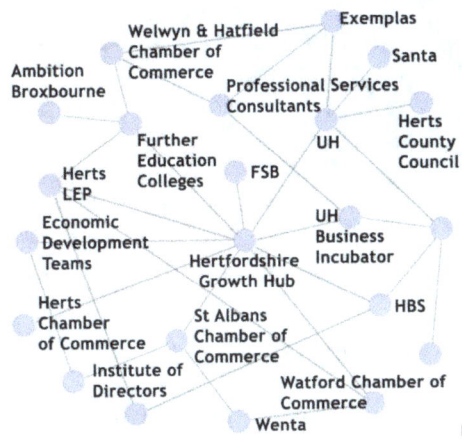

Figure 9: Complex stakeholder engagements[8]

Using primary research data, if local businesses are excluded from the visual representation, the local business ecosystem exemplified in figure

---

[8] The weight and the complexity of each engagement between any two stakeholders is measured based on the number of references each linkage had received, during the primary research stage

9, will have Federation of Small Business in its centre, due to the organisation's high number of interactions with other external stakeholders. If local businesses are collectively considered as a node within the local business ecosystem, then it would be this node in the heart of the local business community, and all other stakeholders will revolve around it.

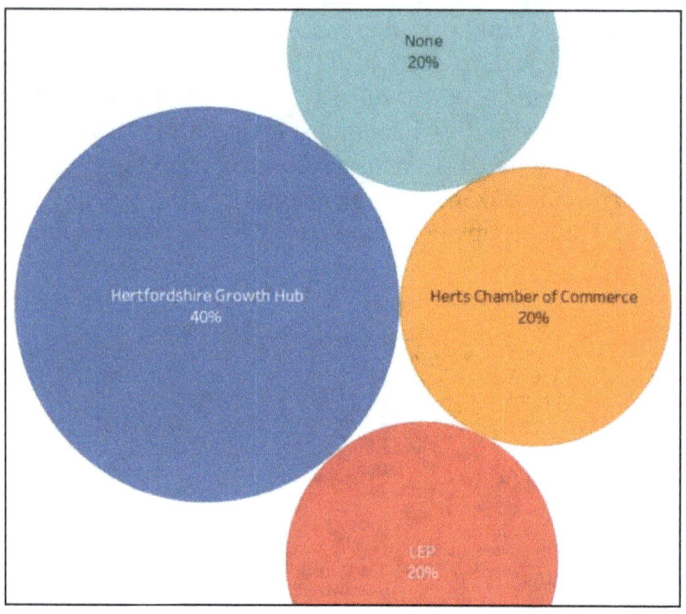

Figure 18: Proportion of influence of central stakeholders[9]

However, when asked to indicate the stakeholder which occupies the centre of the local business ecosystem, the answers point towards Hertfordshire Growth Hub, as shown in figure 18.

---

[9] Proportion from the number of times each external stakeholder has been directly appointed as central to the local business ecosystem

48

1. "(...) the best we've got; they're preparing the local economic strategy (..)" – Participant;

2. "I don't think it's being occupied at the moment in the way in which it should be occupied, but Hertfordshire Growth Hub should occupy it." – Participant.

Yet, according to figure 7 and figure 8, Hertfordshire Growth Hub occupies only the third position if prioritised by the number of linkages it has with other external stakeholders. This information suggests the number of ties is not the only factor which appoints an external stakeholder in the heart of the local business ecosystem.

THE VARIATION OF THE SIZE OF THE ECOSYSTEM

The size of the ecosystem varies between 55 and 800 stakeholders depending on the source of the data considered, i.e. data originating from primary or secondary research. Variation also exists in the number of external stakeholders identified by each interviewee. Primary research did not show a distinction between groups of stakeholders of the same type and individual stakeholders, meaning the collective stakeholder called "Banks" had the same level of influence in the analysis with the stakeholder called "St Albans Chamber of Commerce". However, the former represents several independent banks which are engaging individually with businesses while the latter is a single legal entity. Therefore, it would be assumed that the level of influence banks pose on the local business community is larger compared to the influence St Albans Chamber of Commerce may have.

STAKEHOLDERS' IMPACT ON THE ECOSYSTEM

The stakeholders identified during the primary research fulfil multiple roles for the local business community. Hertfordshire Growth Hub is described as "the first point of call in Herts for any business who needs support or needs to interact with the wider business ecosystem" (Participant) to Pro-connect, described as the "programme that supports creative industries" (Participant); therefore its impact is concentrated on supporting a particular niche. On a different dimension, some stakeholders fulfil roles which involve other stakeholders and not necessarily businesses as it happens with the banks, accountants and professional services consultants about which one interviewee set the expectation that "they should know about the Growth Hub and should advise their client businesses accordingly" (Participant). Primary research identified that the majority of stakeholders fulfil a networking role, positively affecting the local business community by connecting people and institutions as St Albans Business Network is described to provide "networking opportunities for over 3,000 businesses registered; it relies on a high number of micro and small businesses" (Participant). Secondary research offers more in-depth categorisation systems through the use of business directories.

CHALLENGES FELT AT THE BUSINESS LEVEL

A substantial number of challenges were identified during the primary research, excerpting pressure on the business ecosystem but also individual stakeholders. The biggest challenge expressed by businesses refers to the congestion caused by stakeholders, and interviewees describe it with straight-forward phrases such as:

1. "(...) too many people for them (businesses) to interact with (...)" - Participant;

2. "There are too many business support networks in Herts." - Participant;

3. "I don't think it's clear who does what (in the context of external stakeholders) and when and why." - Participant; and

4. "There's no clear catalogue (of stakeholders), and if you're a start-up you might be engaging with the Innovation Hub at the university, or if you're a GSK (i.e. a large organisation) you might be engaging with the CBI or LEP." - Participant.

Figure 10: The primary type of challenges affecting the local business community[10]

The primary research associated the problems affecting Hertfordshire's business community (from figure 10) with the identity of the local stakeholders and identified that the most affected group consists of businesses themselves, as indicated in figure 11. The research findings show that almost all issues felt by the local business community have a certain level of impact on local.

- Business Community
- Hertfordshire Growth Hub
- Herts Chamber of Commerce
- LEP
- Stakeholders
- UH

Figure 11: Most affected stakeholders as a result of the challenges identified in figure 10

---

[10] Length of the bar indicates the intensity with which each issue is affecting the external stakeholder

CHALLENGES PERCEIVED BY BUSINESSES

The primary research took a step further and analysed the problems affecting businesses only (since it is the most affected stakeholders from the local business community). As such, the interview findings revealed:

1. The lack of finance: "(...) (not having) access to funding, cashflow (...)" - Participant;

2. Not having access to adequate skills and resources:

   a. "Massive skills shortages (are) in Hertfordshire" - Participant;

   b. "Herts has a very tight labour market, we've got more or less arguably full employment, some districts have more vacant jobs than unemployed people to fill them; we lose more people commuting out of the county than come into the country; we have an issue around staff and skilled staff" - Participant;

3. Not having enough space to work:

   a. "Good quality employment space due to the shortage and conversion to housing" - Participant;

   b. "Loss and lack of commercial space" - Participant;

4. Lack of knowledge and advice have also been reported as Figure 12 shows.

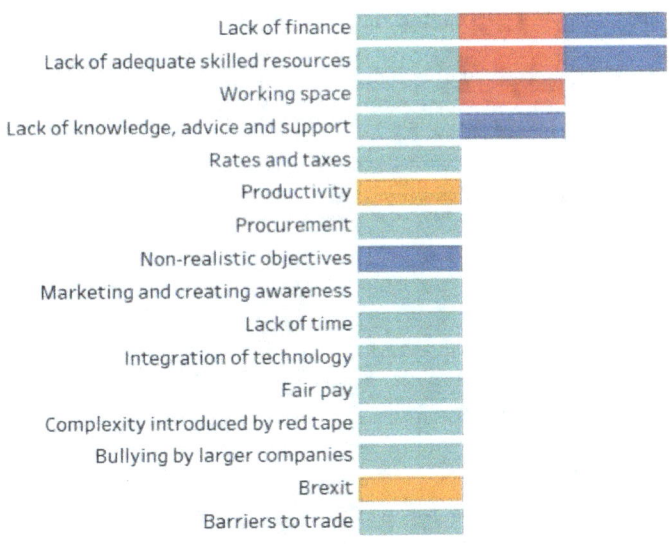

Figure 12: Most pressing challenges affecting businesses

Although five representatives of the local business community were interviewed, the primary research data supplied responses from only four interviewees and as the correlation between figure 12 and figure 13 shows, most of the answers were provided by interviewee 5, which suggests having embedded knowledge and insights obtained using business' lens is a critical factor in understanding the challenges they experience.

Figure 13: Source of the insights for the most pressing challenges affecting businesses

THE LINKAGE BETWEEN HBS AND BUSINESSES

In light with the scope of the research project, the interviews focused on the relationships between HBS and the local small business.

Figure 14: The relationship between the two external stakeholders

The findings suggest there are several misalignments, including HBS's image or how it comes across:

1. "(...) an awareness challenge, i.e. many businesses would not consider approaching a business school for open advice and consultancy." - Participant;

2. "Even if businesses become aware (of HBS), do they understand the true value of working with HBS?" - Participant;

3. "If HBS would have a stronger brand, HBS might have more requests because people might approach the institution more often" - Participant;

4. "(...) re-branding process is needed, improvement strategy to shift the perception of small businesses." - Participant;

The research also touches on HBS's offering: "Micro businesses don't have an idea about HBS as to who they are, or they don't perceive that HBS relates to them" - Participant.

Figure 15: Misalignments reported referring to HBS

The primary data analysed the source of the misalignments reported, and it revealed that almost every interviewee provided a single distinct example of misalignment suggesting a somewhat fragmented perspective and no consensus about the challenges that are frustrating the relationship between the two stakeholders.

Interviewee 1
Interviewee 3
Interviewee 4
Interviewee 5

Figure 16: Sources of the misalignments indicated in figure 15

Interview findings perceive HBS and UH as two distinct potential stakeholders influencing the local business community, although administratively Hertfordshire Business School is incorporated into the University of Hertfordshire. The primary research data shows UH is more likely to have an impact and influence local businesses:

1. "UH has the ambition to become the UK's leading business-facing university" - Participant;

2. "UH has the vision, capabilities, drive, expertise; UH has absolutely everything required to create that central position in the ecosystem" - Participant;

3. "UH provides a talent pipeline, UH provides young students with talent and a degree to join the local businesses" - Participant.

The above interviews also provided a position concerning HBS:

1. "[HBS] doesn't have enough feet on the ground to go out there and provide details about the services HBS provides. HBS can only reach their true potential if they collaborate with other agencies, people on the streets visiting businesses "regularly - Participant;

2. "(HBS is) not broad enough to secure the centre of the local ecosystem, but it is a stakeholder" - Participant.

This information is also backed by secondary research which returns a more comprehensive list of literature references encouraging the industry to engage with the further education institutions and University of Hertfordshire, rather than with Hertfordshire Business School (Tuccillo, 2002; Chartered Association of Business Schools, 2016). In light of the above, the primary research became focused on UH's potential in securing a more central role within Hertfordshire's business ecosystem.

Figure 17: Can HBS and UH be considered stakeholders of the local business ecosystem and can they provide influence

Primary research captured opinions from the five interviewees, seeking to establish which institution from UH or HBS is actively making efforts to secure the central role of the local business ecosystem. The data extracted shows neither stakeholder seeks to achieve the central part of the business ecosystem, as shown in figure 18. Primary research provided a dual perspective about HBS:

1. "[HBS] not looking to become [central to the local business community]; cannot grow; should not compete with existing stakeholders." - Participant;

2. "HBS should be absolutely an exemplar of UH, I don't think it should be the central part [of the local business community]." - Participant;

The interviews extracted positive themes suggesting UH is making steps towards the centre of the business community, by engaging in strategic partnerships:

1. "Business innovation occurs in the university and LEP is trying to promote development in the region so naturally UH must work within LEP in a partnership to promote innovation into the region." - Participant.

HBS	No	
UH	No	
	No in the center, but partnering with the center	
	No in the center, but want to transition into it	

Figure 18: Can HBS and UH be considered stakeholders of the local business ecosystem, and can they provide influence?

KEY AREAS OF IMPROVEMENT

Primary research steered the interview questions around the challenges HBS would be facing if it sought a more central role within the local business ecosystem and learnt that several limitations exist specific to its readiness state. These shortfalls start from not having an adequate framework to enable governance processes and procedures, shortage of qualified staff ("For academic staff, teaching is a big enough priority for them" - Participant). The list of challenges also included legal obstacles which deviate from the academic linear delivery programme and enable an agile consultancy approach (Schwaber, 2009) ("UH does not run like an independent consultancy" - Participant).

Also, slow and ineffective communication channels and operating workflows appear to frustrate external attempts to reach out to internal academics:

1. "Very difficult for businesses to know whom to talk to within the university, because UH is so large and UH covers so many

disciplines, it can feel challenging to want to speak with the person you need" - Participant;

2. "A UH central team should act as a central broker and should have a conversation about what the business needs, their challenges, and how UH might help" - Participant.

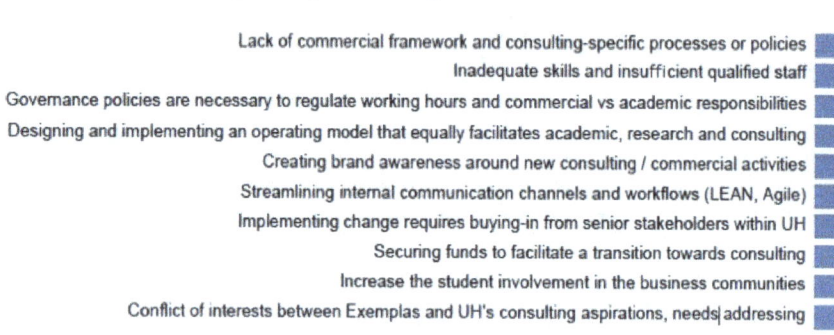

Figure 19: Areas of improvement for HBS

Furthermore, the research found no evidence of preparatory steps to transform the existing HBS operating model:

1. "There is uncertainty about whether competitive consultancy capabilities are available within UH." - Participant;

2. "For UH to compete with boutique consultancies it would be a logistical challenge." - Participant.

The research revealed complexities referring to the working hours of UH staff, given academics are pre-allocated at maximum utilisation to academic work:

1. "It is difficult to get staff willing to give extra time (to consultancy work) because they want to teach" - Participant;

2. "UH does not have a dedicated team to deliver consultancy work" - Participant).

Primary research also revealed the existence of a subsidiary of UH, called Exemplas which did not emerge in the secondary research and which acts entirely on a commercial business model. According to research data, Exemplas is effectively a direct competitor of what HBS is trying to become. Primary research finds:

1. "The subsidiary sits entirely under UH" - Participant;

2. "They're almost competitors of UH in terms of consultancy services" - Participant.

Findings originating from primary research also revealed funding challenges for non-research activities: "A lot of UH funding is research first, business impact second" - Participant. Primary research also found bureaucratic barriers obstructing community engagements ("De-risking internal aspects of UH (is necessary) to allow it to be more entrepreneurial, to allow it to interact with the broader business community, to offer more tangible benefits" - Participant. Research also identified, that steer from UH leadership is needed to provide a vision, method and tools to achieve a transition towards consultancy: "We need guidance at the university level as to what is the most successful methodology for getting academics to do consultancy work" - Participant.

POSITION OF UH IN THE BUSINESS ECOSYSTEM

According to the primary research University of Hertfordshire currently, mainly trains and provides resources ("UH provides a talent pipeline, UH provides young students with talent and a degree to join the local businesses" - Participant). UH would like to "move into consultancy" (Participant), however, either due to branding shortfall ("if UH would have a stronger brand, UH might get more requests because people might approach UH more often" - Participant) or misalignments between the offering and the market demand UH only secures the 8th position in terms of the linkages formed with other external stakeholders. Assuming a shift is achieved and UH will tailor its service offerings to suit the business community needs it would be sufficient to align the institution on a refreshing path which can lead to its objective of becoming more central to the local business community.

Several interview responses indicated the school might not be able to deliver other activities than timetabled academic ones, due to legal-employment constraints.

The primary research found it is less likely that local businesses approach UH for help before reaching out to other external stakeholders such as Herts Chamber of Commerce, Wenta, Hertfordshire Growth Hub, Federation of Small Business, Hertfordshire LEP and Welwyn & Hatfield Chamber of Commerce. This information suggests that UH must open up to the industry through a business unit or department, through which it must provide at least the same level of services these other external organisations are offering. In doing so, UH will secure a share from the market, which will leverage and shift its position more towards the centre of the local business ecosystem. This data requires UH to study the service offering of other institutions and process the relevant value proposition as well as unique selling points and combine findings with strategic differentiators specific to UH, to develop a sustainable competitive advantage and establish themselves as a reliable delivery partner with both academic and professional services.

The next section will blend information from the literature reviewed, with the research findings seeking to conclude for HBS's objective.

CONCLUSIONS & RECOMMENDATIONS

THE BUSINESS ECOSYSTEM

The literature reviewed defined the concept of a business ecosystem and detailed how it should look for the County of Hertfordshire. In doing so, it identified eight key external stakeholders known to influence the business ecosystem, also known as a business community (figure 2 from section external stakeholders). However, primary research identified 55 influential organisations, while secondary research estimated 800 entities including groups, high street banks and other organisations who can provide steer and influence the way businesses to operate (figure 6 from the section: The size of the business ecosystem). Having a total number of external stakeholders in the region of 800 makes very difficult for a micro business to know which stakeholder is best to approach, to learn about a particular service or to scan the service offering of multiple stakeholders.

The "congestion of stakeholders" reported by interviewees, affects the business community in several ways including causing unclarity in terms of the role and responsibilities of each stakeholder, a phenomenon described within the Stakeholder Theory (Volkmann et al., 2017). This condition is not only leading to a lack of clarity in terms of "who does what, when and why" (Participant), as primary research revealed, but also it becomes unclear whether the advice received by one stakeholder is as valuable or even relevant compared to the information which a second stakeholder may provide, should the enquiring organisation know about the latter's existence and offers. Although there is no centralised catalogue of external stakeholders (Link, 2014) which one start-up, for example, can navigate or enquire for the best source of knowledge in a particular subject, primary research revealed stakeholders had developed a reputation of contributing to specific sectors or being able to advise the precise type of businesses.

THE CENTER OF THE BUSINESS ECOSYSTEM

Another preposition drawn from the research combined with the literature reviewed shows Hertfordshire business ecosystem lacks a centralised, trusted, updated mechanism in which each external stakeholder can clarify its offer and list of operational capabilities. Another use of this service is to allow businesses to access this repository of information in a decluttered fashion, to enquire and receive direction as suggested through Stakeholder Theory (Volkmann et al., 2017). This mechanism must not necessarily be a technological one, as it can also be delivered by personnel in a variety of ways (i.e. over the phone, email or face-to-face) and with various frequencies (repetitively or as a one-off). Given HBS' objective of becoming central to the local business ecosystem, the research project recommends that the business school steps in to fill this gap. Also, it aims to evaluate whether this transition is doable or otherwise and how should HBS change its business model to accommodate the new duties towards the local business community.

Naturally, the next phase of the research project was to investigate who occupies the core of the Hertfordshire business ecosystem, knowing HBS aims at transitioning to it. Existing literature reveals business schools around the UK are encouraged to seek to undertake this transition and examples were found where various business schools engaged with businesses mainly to expose students to real-life challenges and enable them to gain hands-on experience before their graduation (Universities UK, 2016; Chartered Association of Business Schools, 2016). However, primary research revealed the most relevant remarks made during the interview sessions pointed towards Hertfordshire Growth Hub stating it currently represents "the first point of call in Hertfordshire for any business who needs support and to interact with the wider business ecosystem" (Participant) making it a compelling candidate for the heart of the business community.

Despite aspiring to be a "leading business-facing university" (Participant), the research finds that neither UH or HBS have secured a central role for the local business community. It is acknowledged that powerful incentives exist, stimulated by literature and industry papers, encouraging business schools to undertake a central role. However, in the case of Hertfordshire County, it appears this function is delivered collectively by Hertfordshire Growth Hub, Hertfordshire LEP, Herts Chamber of Commerce and the Federation of Small Businesses.

CURRENT CONDITION

Research shows HBS is perceived as excelling at providing academic expertise, making a case for a business model which is prioritising academic teaching as represented in figure 4 from section BUSINESS SCHOOLS, in the detriment of business community engagement.

HBS is not positioned in the centre of the local business ecosystem, as seen in figure 9 from section STAKEHOLDER RELATIONSHIPS. However, it does link to the community of local businesses as shown in figure 22, and it has the potential to transition to a more central position if it leverages its ability to tailor its business model and addresses the challenges the local business community are signalling.

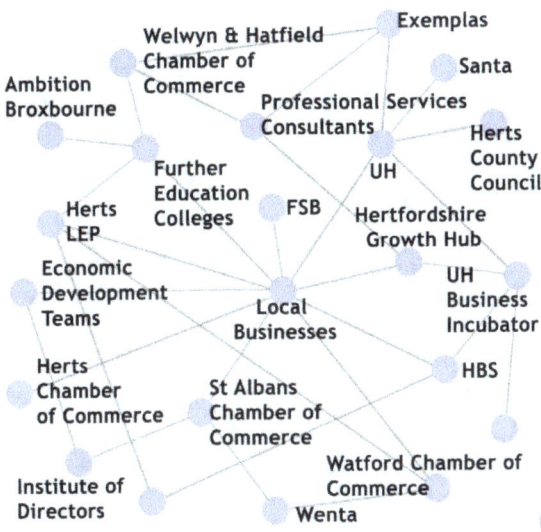

Figure 22: HBS' position within the local business ecosystem, with respect to local businesses

OPPORTUNITY

Research shows HBS is perceived as being "ambitious at engaging with businesses" (Participant) while UH is known to "encourage entrepreneurship in the local business community" (Participant), setting up the premises that Hertfordshire's only higher education institution "aims to create strategic partnerships" (Participant), which can lead to opportunities of "a collaboration between businesses and stakeholders" (Participant).

However, primary research indicates several challenges the university is faced with, including "lack of offering awareness [within the business community]" (Participant) and "misalignments between UH offering and local business needs" (Participant). These shortfalls are amplified by the lack of awareness about the university's brand and its commercial services. This phenomenon reveals the opportunity for HBS to deep dive into the business community to study and thoroughly understand the main challenges businesses are faced with, which were identified during the primary research and structured in two categories:

1. Fundamental enablers for local companies, which represent avenues HBS could potentially engage with the business community to offer support:

    a. Resources;

    b. Financials;

    c. Working space.

2. Specialised advice support lines actively sought by the local businesses:

    a. Accounting;

    b. Productivity;

    c. Procurement;

    d. Marketing;

    e. Technology;

f.   Red tape;

g.   Brexit;

h.   Environmental approvals and permits.

Research shows that if HBS is to provide the above services as part of a new target business model to local businesses, the business school will receive the right credentials which will reposition it in the heart of the local business community.

The research also shows that HBS has the opportunity to tailor its services to make them more relevant for micro and small businesses. After adjusting the offering, HBS has another chance to advertise them using a brand and marketing package which helps organisations understand the value in working with university staff and students, to create trusted long term relationships and lead to an overall change in the perception of the academic institution and its contribution to Hertfordshire's business ecosystem.

TRANSITION

Primary research revealed that the university needs to streamline its internal communication channels and workflows. This process can be achieved by implementing modern operational methodologies such as Lean (Jackson, 1996) and Agile (Schwaber, 2009) recommended for creating opportunities for operational efficiencies, increasing transparency and shrinking the number of steps between setting an objective and signing it as complete. This simplification will enable HBS to coordinate the linkages observed within the university, described in the literature review as being specific to the Systems Theory (Skyttner, 2001), which primary research perceives at the moment as rarely controllable.

The research shows that increasing the level of control, transparency and flexibility within UH will also enable the institution to set out a new operating model which is not focused only on teaching (as the current one is), but which addresses the challenges identified in this research project. These opportunities for improvement include "de-risking internal aspects of the university to allow it to be more entrepreneurial" (Participant). Also, these changes will enable UH to engage as part of its academic programmes with local industry, to provide professional and academic expertise while shifting the public perception about HBS.

While undertaking this continuous engagement exercise between itself and the local business community, HBS will begin to understand the challenges and sources of potential improvements which businesses will need. In doing so UH will be able to tailor its service offering to support micro and small businesses, as well as adjusting the academic curriculum and the portfolio of degrees and educational programmes including apprenticeships or technical degrees (Cantor, 1993) based on the relevant industry resource necessities.

The research shows that another aspect which enables HBS to undertake this transition refers to its brand and how the business community is perceiving it. Data from the interviews show HBS is currently seen as an institution concerned with teaching, and therefore it should seek to move more towards consulting, it should follow Examplas' model which according to the primary research is a subsidiary of UH that delivers consultancy services. Examplas, has its operating model and brand which does not include visual or branding components used by UH or HBS.

According to Stakeholder Theory (Bischoff, Volkmann and Audretsch, 2017), to undertake this transition HBS must first obtain the buying from stakeholders who are likely to act later as catalysts or enablers during the course of the transition. The list of stakeholders includes both internal staff and external entities. Although this paper does not name them, it makes strong references towards the need for cross-collaboration across all schools within UH, as well as external stakeholders and alumni identified during the primary research that HBS already engages. These steering engagements between stakeholders must be recurring and as primary research identified, must oversee the maturity of the transition in its entirety from securing funding for staffing and training up to industry liaison and annual curriculum revisions based on external factors (Marmol, Feys and Probert, 2015), PESTLE, Porter 5 Forces and industry changes.

66

By undergoing the above transition and creating several strategic partnerships with existing established external stakeholders, the research project finds that HBS is expected on mid to long term to shift towards the centre of the local business ecosystem.

If HBS is to incorporate the above research findings into a new business model, it will enable the business school to provide adequate services well sought by Herts business community which will then provide the organisation with the right credentials, and it will grant it the primary position within Hertfordshire business ecosystem.

FURTHER RESEARCH

More research is necessary to analyse other business schools and the way they position themselves in different counties and other business communities across the UK. Extrapolating the findings from this paper to other universities and business schools as well as the recommendations made to HBS may lead to errors and incompatibilities between Hertfordshire ecosystem and other business communities.

The research project recommends a much more comprehensive series of interviews to be conducted with each external stakeholder identified in the secondary research of this paper (around 800) to construct a map as accurate as possible, of the local business and adjust the number of resources allocated for HBS transition.

REFERENCES

1. Arruda, C., Nogueira, V.S., & Costa, V. (2014). The Brazilian entrepreneurial ecosystem of start-ups: An analysis of entrepreneurship determinants in Brazil as seen from the OECD pillars. Journal of Entrepreneurship and Innovation Management, 2(3), 17–57.
2. Audretsch, D. B., Falck, O., Feldman, M. P., & Heblich, S. (2011). Local entrepreneurship in context. Regional Studies, 46(3), 379–389.
3. Bakhtiar Rana, M. and Allen, M. (2018). Business Systems Perspective on Entrepreneurship. Manchester: Research Gate.
4. Barro, R. (2001). Determinants of economic growth. Cambridge, Mass.: MIT Press.
5. BBC News. (2019). 'Worst yet to come' in council cuts. [online] Available at: https://www.bbc.co.uk [Accessed 27 Jan. 2019].
6. Ben Letaifa, S., Gratacap, A., Isckia, T. and Pesqueux, Y. (2013). Understanding business ecosystems. Bruxelles: De Boeck.
7. Bertalanffy, L. (2015). General system theory. New York: Braziller.
8. Berthod, O. (2018). Institutional theory of organizations. Berlin: Global Encyclopedia of Public Administration, Public Policy, and Governance.
9. Biopark.co.uk. (2018). Hertfordshire LEP. [online] Available at: http://www.biopark.co.uk [Accessed 26 Dec. 2018].
10. Bischoff, K., Volkmann, C. and Audretsch, D. (2017). Stakeholder collaboration in entrepreneurship education: an analysis of the entrepreneurial ecosystems of European higher educational institutions. New York: Springer Science Business Media.
11. Blackburn, M. (2017). Business Schools Delivering Value to Local and Regional Economies. London: Chartered Association of Business Schools.
12. Bonnafous-Boucher, M. and Rendtorff, J. (2016). Stakeholder Theory. Cham: Springer International Publishing.
13. British Business Bank. (2018). Homepage - British Business Bank. [online] Available at: https://www.british-business-bank.co.uk [Accessed 27 Dec. 2018].

14. Brown, M. (2018). How Important Are Small Businesses to Local Economies? [online] Smallbusiness.chron.com. Available at: https://smallbusiness.chron.com [Accessed 20 Jan. 2019].
15. Bryman, A. (2012) Social Research Methods. Oxford: Oxford University Press.
16. Business Insider (2018). The 13 best business schools in the UK, according to the Financial Times. [online] Available at: http://uk.businessinsider.com/ [Accessed 31 Oct. 2018].
17. Cantor, J. (1993). Promoting Collaboration with Business, Labour and the Community for Workforce Training. Univ. P. of America.
18. Carayannis, E., Dagnino, G., Alvarez, S. and Faraci, R. (2018). Entrepreneurial ecosystems and the diffusion of start-ups. Massachusetts: Edward Elgar Publishing.
19. Carayannis, E., Provance, M. and Grigoroudis, E. (2016). Entrepreneurship ecosystems: an agent-based simulation approach. New York: Springer Science.
20. Cavalcante, S., Kesting, P., and Ulhøi, J. (2011) Business model dynamics and innovation: (re)establishing the missing linkages. Management Decision, 49, 1327– 1342.
21. Chambers, H. (2019). Hertfordshire Chamber of Commerce. [online] Hertschamber.com. Available at: http://www.hertschamber.com/ [Accessed 6 Jan. 2019].
22. Chartered Association of Business Schools (2016). Business Schools Delivering Value to Local and Regional Economies. London: Chartered Association of Business Schools (CABS).
23. Chartered Association of Business Schools (2018). BEIS Business Productivity Review - Response from the Chartered Association of Business Schools. London: Chartered Association of Business Schools. ⌈¹⌉SEP⌋
24. Chartered Association of Business Schools (2018). BEIS Business Productivity Review. London: Chartered Association of Business Schools.
25. Chartered Association of Business Schools. UK Business Schools and International Student Recruitment: Trends, challenges and the case for change. [online] London: Chartered Association of Business Schools. Available at: http://charteredabs.org [Accessed 26 Nov. 2018].

26. Chron. (2019). What Are Internal & External Environmental Factors That Affect Business? [online] Available at: https://smallbusiness.chron.com [Accessed 5 Mar. 2019].
27. Collaborative business ecosystems and virtual enterprises. (2013). New York: Springer-Verlag New York.
28. Collinson, S. (2017). Business Schools Delivering Value to Local and Regional Economies. London: Chartered Association of Business Schools.
29. Companies House (2018). Companies register activities 2017 to 2018. [online] London: Companies House. Available at: https://www.gov.uk [Accessed 28 Dec. 2018].
30. Cornuel, E. (2005). Vision for business schools. Bradford, England: Emerald Group Publishing.
31. Creswell, J. (2018). A concise introduction to mixed methods research.
32. Crotty, M. (1998). The foundations of social research. London: Sage Publications.
33. Deloitte Insights. (2019). Introduction: Business ecosystems come of age. [online] Available at: https://www2.deloitte.com [Accessed 5 Mar. 2019].
34. Department for Business, Energy & Industrial Strategy (2018). Business Productivity Review - Government call for evidence. London: Department for Business, Energy & Industrial Strategy.
35. Department of Education (2017). Hertfordshire Area Review - Final Report. London: Department of Education.
36. Dubini, P. (1989). The influence of motivations and environment on business start-ups: Some hints for public policies. Journal of Business Venturing, 4(1), 11-26.
37. Ecclesiastical Insurance Office (2018). Looking to the future – what is the likely impact of Brexit on education establishments? Gloucester: Ecclesiastical Insurance Office PLC.
38. Eduniversal-ranking.com. (2018). University and business school ranking in United Kingdom. [online] Available at: http://www.eduniversal-ranking.com/ [Accessed 20 Oct. 2018].
39. Enterprise Research center. (2018). It's time for Britain's Brexit negotiators 'educated' themselves on the needs of small business -

Enterprise Research center. [online] Available at: https://www.enterpriseresearch.ac.uk [Accessed 18 Oct. 2018].

40. Entrepreneur Handbook. (2019). List of small business grants in the UK. [online] Available at: https://entrepreneurhandbook.co.uk [Accessed 21 Jan. 2019].

41. Fayolle, A. (2018). A research agenda for entrepreneurship education. Emlyon: Elgar.

42. Feldman, M. (2001). The entrepreneurial event revisited: Firm formation in a regional context. Industrial and Corporate Change, 10(4), 861–891.

43. Feldman, M., & Zoller, T. D. (2012). Dealmakers in place: Social capital connections in regional entrepreneurial economies. Regional Studies, 46(1), 23–37.

44. Feldman, M., Francis, J., & Bercovitz, J. (2005). Creating a cluster while building a firm: Entrepreneurs and the formation of industrial clusters. Regional Studies, 39(1), 129-141.

45. Forbes.com. (2018). 12 Challenges Start-up Culture Must Overcome in Order to Thrive in 2017. [online] Available at: https://www.forbes.com/ [Accessed 30 Dec. 2018].

46. Forbes.com. (2019). Lifestyle Businesses. [online] Available at: https://www.forbes.com/ [Accessed 10 Mar. 2019].

47. Foreman, J. (2019). Chaos vs. Control. [online] HuffPost. Available at: https://www.huffpost.com [Accessed 6 Apr. 2019].

48. Foss, N. J., Lyngsie, J. and Zahra, S. A. (2013) The role of external knowledge sources and organizational design in the process of opportunity exploitation. Strategic Management Journal 34(12): 1453-1471.

49. Freeman, R. (2010). Strategic management: A stakeholder approach. Cambridge: Cambridge University Press.

50. Freeman, R., Harrison, J. S., Wicks, A. C., Parmar, B. L., & De Colle, S. (2014). Stakeholder theory: The

51. Freitag, A. (2015). Applying Business Capabilities in a Corporate Buyer M & A Process. Wiesbaden: Springer Gabler.

52. Fsb.org.uk. (2019). Can business schools help take your business to the next level? [online] Available at: https://www.fsb.org.uk [Accessed 5 Mar. 2019].

53. Ft.com-2. (2018). Number of UK start-ups rises to new record. [online] Available at: https://www.ft.com [Accessed 25 Dec. 2018].

54. Ft.com. (2018). FT European Business School Rankings 2018 | Financial Times. [online] Available at: https://www.ft.com [Accessed 2 Dec. 2018].

55. Gourd, J. and Matthey, J. (2018). The Hertfordshire Economy.

56. Gov.uk-2. (2018). The Hertfordshire Start-up Programme. [online] Available at: https://www.gov.uk [Accessed 27 Dec. 2018].

57. Gov.uk. (2018). Finance and support for your business - GOV.UK [online] Available at: https://www.gov.uk [Accessed 14 Sep. 2018].

58. Grant Thornton UK LLP (2017). Hertfordshire Ltd 2017. St Albans: Grant Thornton UK LLP.

59. Hamilton, E. (2016). Business Schools Delivering Value to Local and Regional Economies. London: Chartered Association of Business Schools.

60. Helyer, R. and Lee, D., 2014. The role of work experience in the future employability of higher education graduates. Higher Education Quarterly, 68(3), pp.348-372.

61. Hertfordshire County Council (2018). A Draft Summary of the Hertfordshire context - Growth, Challenges & Opportunities. [online] London: Hertfordshire County Council. Available at: https://www.hertfordshire.gov.uk [Accessed 20 Oct. 2018].

62. Hertfordshire LEP. (2015). Economic Overview | Herts LEP. [online] Available at: https://www.hertfordshirelep.com [Accessed 29 Dec. 2018].

63. Hertfordshire LEP. (2019). Funding | Herts LEP. [online] Available at: https://www.hertfordshirelep.com [Accessed 21 Jan. 2019].

64. Hertfordshire Local Council. (2019). Business. [online] Available at: https://www.hertfordshire.gov.uk [Accessed 21 Jan. 2019].

65. Hertfordshire Local Enterprise Partnership (2018). Releasing our Potential - Hertfordshire Skills Strategy to 2020. [online] Welwyn Garden City: Hertfordshire Local Enterprise Partnership. Available at: https://www.hertfordshirelep.com [Accessed 25 Apr. 2018].

66. Hertfordshire Ltd. (2017). St Albans: Grant Thornton.

67. Hesa.ac.uk. (2018). Higher Education Student Statistics: UK, 2016/17 - Student numbers and characteristics | HESA. [online] Available at: https://www.hesa.ac.uk [Accessed 15 Apr. 2018].

68. Hooley, T., Mellors-Bourne, R. and Sutton, M., 2013. Early evaluation of Unistats: user experiences. UK Higher Education Funding Bodies.

69. Ivascu, L., Cirjaliu, B. and Draghici, A. (2015). Business model for the university-industry collaboration in open innovation. Rome: ScienceDirect.

70. Ivory, D., Miskell, D., Shipton, D., White, D., Moeslein, P. and Neely, P. (2018). The Future of Business Schools in the UK. Coventry: University of Warwick.

71. Jackson, T. (1996). Implementing a lean management system. Productivity Press.

72. Judith Bernard, A. (2012). Change Management in Academia. Worcester: Worcester Polytechnic Institute.

73. Julien, P. A. (2007). A theory of local entrepreneurship in the knowledge economy. Cheltenham, UK: Edward Elgar.

74. Karhiniemi, M. (2009). Creating and Sustaining Successful Business Ecosystems. Information Systems Science Master's thesis. Karhiniemi: Department of Business Technology.

75. Kruss, G. (2006). Working partnerships in higher education, industry and innovation. Cape Town: HSRC.

76. Lexicon.ft.com. (2019). Business Ecosystem Definition from Financial Times Lexicon. [online] Available at: http://lexicon.ft.com/ [Accessed 5 Jan. 2019].

77. Lima, E. (2017). Systemic approaches to understand entrepreneurship and strategic management. São Paulo: Cairn.

78. Link, A. (2014). Public Support of Innovation in Entrepreneurial Firms. Cheltenham: Edward Elgar Publishing.

79. London, M. (1995). Achieving performance excellence in university administration. Westport, Conn.: Praeger.

80. Malecki, E. J. (1997). Entrepreneurs, networks, and economic development: A review of recent research. In J. Katz (Ed.), Advances in entrepreneurship, firm emergence, and growth (Vol. 3, pp. 57–118). Greenwich, CT: JAI Press.

81. Management Learning (2014). Relevance or 'reelevate'? How university business schools can add value through reflexively learning from strategic partnerships with business. Glasgow: Management Learning.

82. Mansfield, N. (2000). Subjectivity. New York: New York University Press.
83. Marmol, T., Feys, B. and Probert, C. (2015). PESTLE analysis. 50Minutes.
84. Mason, R. (2015). The Impact of Business School Research: Economic and Social Benefits. London: Chartered Association of Business Schools.
85. Maxwell, J. (2008). A realistic approach to qualitative design. London: SAGE.
86. Maxwell, J. (2009). Qualitative research design. Thousand Oaks, Calif: Sage.
87. Miller, K., McAdam, M. and McAdam, R. (2019). The changing university business model: a stakeholder perspective. Belfast: RADMA and John Wiley & Sons Ltd.
88. Momani, B. and Malecki, M. (2012). The global reach of management consulting firms. Occasional paper. Canada: University of Waterloo.
89. Neck, H. M., Meyer, G. D., Cohen, B., & Corbett, A. C. (2004). An entrepreneurial system view of new venture creation. Journal of Small Business Management, 42(2), 190–208.
90. Network, Q. (2019). Current trends in higher education today and its outlook - QS WOWNEWS. [online] QS WOWNEWS. Available at: https://qswownews.com/ [Accessed 19 Jan. 2019].
91. OECD. and Oecd Publishing, P. (1999). Business Incubation. Paris: Organisation for Economic Co-operation and Development.
92. ONS. (2019). Office for National Statistics. [online] Available at: https://www.ons.gov.uk [Accessed 8 Apr. 2019].
93. Osterwalder, A. and Pigneur, Y. (2013). Business Model Generation. New York, NY: John Wiley & Sons.
94. Paton, S., Chia, R. and Burt, G. (2014). Relevance or 'reelevate'? How university business schools can add value through reflexively learning from strategic partnerships with business. Glasgow: Management Learning.
95. Patton, D., & Kenney, M. (2005). The spatial configuration of the entrepreneurial support network for the semiconductor industry. R&D Management, 35(1), 1–17.

96. Peters, G. (2010). Institutional Theory: Problems and Prospects. Pittsburgh: University of Pittsburgh.

97. Pitelis, C. (2012). Clusters, entrepreneurial ecosystem co-creation, and appropriability: A conceptual framework. Industrial and Corporate Change, 21(6), 1359–1388.

98. Pop, A. (2018). Best 10 Business Schools in the UK - Top MBAs Worldwide in 2018 - MastersPortal.com. [online] Mastersportal.com. Available at: https://www.mastersportal.com/ [Accessed 5 Oct. 2018].

99. Provance, M., Donnellyb, R. and Carayannisb, E. (2011). Institutional influences on business model choice by new ventures in the micro generated energy industry. Energy Policy. Elsevier.

100. Pulla, S. and Schissel, B. (2018). Applied Interdisciplinarity in Scholar Practitioner Programs. Cham: Springer International Publishing.

101. Rankings.ft.com. (2018). Business school rankings from the Financial Times - FT.com. [online] Available at: http://rankings.ft.com/ [Accessed 2 Dec. 2018].

102. Ridenour, C. and Newman, I. (2008). Mixed methods research. Carbondale: Southern Illinois University Press.

103. Rothschild, M. (2004). Bionomics. Washington: BeardBooks.

104. Samovar, L. A., Porter, R. E. and McDaniel, E. R. (2014) Intercultural communication: a reader. USA: Cenage Learning.

105. Saunders, M., Lewis, P. and Thornhill, A. (2012). Research methods for business students. Harlow [etc.]: Pearson Education Limited.

106. Schwaber, K. (2009). Agile Project Management with Scrum. New York: O'Reilly Media, Inc.

107. Schwartz-Salant, N. (2017). Order-Disorder Paradox. North Atlantic Books.

108. SemLEP. (2019). Local Growth Fund. [online] Available at: https://www.semlep.com [Accessed 21 Jan. 2019].

109. Skyttner, L. (2008). General Systems Theory. Singapore: World Scientific, pp.110-118.

110. Smerdon, B., Kim, K. and Alfeld, C. (2018). Career and College Readiness and Success for All Students.

111. Spekman, R., Wittmannrt, M. and Lambe, J. (2008). Social Exchange Theory and Research on Business-to-Business Relational Exchange. Journal of Business-to-Business Marketing. New York.
112. STANTA. (2019). Networking Groups - STANTA. [online] Available at: https://stanta.co.uk [Accessed 18 Mar. 2019].
113. Startup Genome Project (2012). Startup Ecosystem Report 2012. https://goo.gl/F3Ta7P accessed 14 June 2015. state of the art. New York: Cambridge University Press.
114. Stebbins, R. (2001). Exploratory research in the social sciences. Thousand Oaks, Calif.: Sage Publications.
115. Sturdy, A. and O'Mahoney, J. (2018). Explaining national variation in the use of management consulting knowledge. SAGE Publications.
116. Teece, D. J. (2010) Business models, business strategy and innovation. Long Range Planning, 43, 172–194.
117. The Economist. (2018). Growing competition between universities is changing student life. [online] Available at: https://www.economist.com/ [Accessed 27 Jan. 2019].
118. Tihanyi, L., Devinney, T. and Pedersen, T. (2012). Institutional theory in international business and management. United Kingdom (Ireland): Emerald Group Publishing Limited.
119. Top Universities. (2019). Top Universities. [online] Available at: https://www.topuniversities.com [Accessed 6 Mar. 2019].
120. Tuccillo, J. (2002). New business models for a new economy. Chicago, IL: Dearborn Real Estate Education.
121. UCAS. (2018). UCAS - University of Hertfordshire. [online] Available at: https://digital.ucas.com [Accessed 6 Jan. 2019].
122. UK Commission for Employment and Skills (2014). UK labour market projections: 2012 to 2022. London: UK Commission for Employment and Skills.
123. UK Government (2017). Industrial Strategy. London: UK Government.
124. Ukcitynetworking.com. (2019). Networking in Hertfordshire. Networks and networking resources in Hertfordshire. [online] Available at: https://www.ukcitynetworking.com [Accessed 18 Mar. 2019].

125. Unistats.ac.uk. (2018). Business Administration - Unistats. [online] Available at: https://unistats.ac.uk [Accessed 11 May 2018].
126. Universities UK (2016). HIGHER EDUCATION IN ENGLAND: PROVISION, SKILLS AND GRADUATES. London: Universities UK.
127. Universities UK. (2016). The economic impact of UK higher education institutions. London: Universities UK.
128. University of Edinburgh Business School (2017). The Relational Organization of Entrepreneurial Ecosystems. Edinburgh: University of Edinburgh Business School.
129. University of Hertfordshire (2015). Hertfordshire Business Skills Gaps Survey 2014-15. Hatfield: University of Hertfordshire.
130. University of Hertfordshire 3. (2018). Hertfordshire Business School. [online] Available at: https://www.herts.ac.uk [Accessed 29 Oct. 2018].
131. University of Hertfordshire 4. (2019). What is a degree apprenticeship? [online] Available at: https://www.herts.ac.uk/ [Accessed 21 Jan. 2019].
132. University of Hertfordshire. (2019). Schools of study. [online] Available at: https://www.herts.ac.uk [Accessed 6 Jan. 2019].
133. Van der Borgh, M., Cloodt, M., & Romme, A.G.L. (2012). Value creation by knowledge–based ecosystems: Evidence from a field study. R&D Management, 42(2), 150–169.
134. Wedge, P. and Prosser, H. (2009). Born to Fail? London: Jessica Kingsley Publishers.
135. Weinberg, G. (2001). An introduction to general systems thinking. New York, NY: Dorset House.
136. Wilson, T. (2012). A Review of Business–Industry Collaboration. London: Department for Business, I.S.
137. Wolfe, D. (2005). The role of universities in regional development and cluster formation. In G. Jones, P. McCarney, & M. Skolnik (Eds.), Creating knowledge, strengthening nations (pp. 167-194). Toronto: University of Toronto Press.
138. World Economic Forum (2013). Entrepreneurial ecosystems around the globe and company growth dynamics (industry agenda). Geneva: World Economic Forum.

139. WU. (2019). University rankings and reviews. [online] Available at: https://www.whatuni.com [Accessed 6 Mar. 2019].
140. Yazdani, B. (2012). Defining the role of business schools. Nottingham.
141. Yin, R. (2008). Case study research. Thousand Oaks, California: SAGE.
142. Zahra, S. (2015). Corporate entrepreneurship as knowledge creation and conversion: the role of entrepreneurial hubs. Minneapolis, USA: Springer Link.